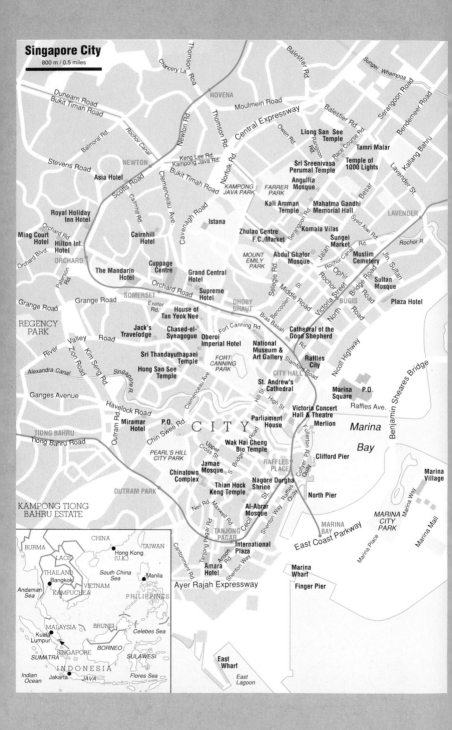

Singapore City

800 m / 0.5 miles

Selamat Datang!

Imagine you have a friend in Singapore, someone who can show you round the island state, someone who knows where to go, what to see, where to buy what, and perhaps more importantly, where and what to eat. For Singapore is renowned, not only as an interesting melting pot of Asian culture and a great place for a shopping spree, but also as one of the culinary centres of Asia.

Your guide, Marianne Rankin, has lived in Asia for fifteen years, fourteen of them in Singapore. She has taught, translated and interpreted, and also written for a local tourist magazine during that time. Let her show you the Singapore she knows and loves, the Singapore often missed by tourists on short stop-overs on the way to more far flung destinations in Asia and the Antipodes.

This guide is for the active traveller who wants to understand and appreciate the history and culture of Singapore and to see as much as possible, making the most of even a short stay here.

Marianne begins by tracing the history of the island from its early days as a vital point on the lucrative trade route from the Pacific to the Indian Ocean, to today's metropolis, the busiest port in the world, where the citizens enjoy one of the highest standards of living in Asia.

She then takes you on two full-day itineraries to familiarise you with the island. On the first day you gain an insight into the development of Singapore with a look at the colonial heart of the city and the business district, followed by a boat trip around the harbour and offshore islands. The Singapore River and part of old Chinatown complete this overview, and the day ends in the glittering shops and restaurants of Orchard Road.

The next day you are introduced to the people of Singapore, to the lives and religions of the three main racial groups, the Chinese, Indians and Malays.

Then just select what interests you from the itineraries which Marianne has suggested but remember that they are simply suggestions to help you to make your own discovery of the fascinating island city state of Singapore. You'll soon find that there is far more here than first meets the eye.

Selamat Datang! Welcome!

Insight Pocket Guide:

SINGAPORE

First Edition

© 1991 APA Publications (HK) Ltd.

All Rights Reserved

Printed in Singapore by

Höfer Press (Pte) Ltd

Fax: 65-861 6438

INSIGHT *pocket* GUIDES

SINGAPORE

Written by	**Marianne Rankin**
Directed by	**Hans Hofer**
Design Concept by	**V. Barl**
Art Direction by	**Karen Hoisington**
Photography by	**Ingo Jezierski**
Editorial Director	**Michael Stachels**

INSIGHT *pocket* GUIDES

Contents

Maps

Like so many expatriate women, I came to Singapore through no choice of my own, and with no idea how long I would spend here. My husband was transferred here, so I found myself with a new place to explore and a new life ahead of me.

Fourteen years later, we're still here and I'm still discovering fascinating nooks and crannies hidden behind the glittering facades of Singapore's new hotels and shopping centres.

As I had lived in the jungle in Asia before coming here, the first attraction of the place for me was, in fact, the sophisticated side. The spacious lounges, bars and discos of gleaming new hotels, the myriads of restaurants serving delectable dishes from all over the world and of course all those tantalising shops, selling tempting treasures from every corner of the globe were manna to me.

Later, I became more interested in Singapore's past and in the variety of people and cultures blending into everyday life here. I began to read the history of the nation and to look more deeply at what I saw around me. Gradually I began to understand more about this island, so worldly and sophisticated on the surface, so complex and full of superstition beneath.

At first I found the place noisy, and living in a flat very hard to adjust to. I wondered how to get to know the locals. I was also determined to avoid the expat ladies' cocoon of coffee mornings and clubs.

So I worked. Teaching English as a Foreign Language gave me a chance to listen to the life stories of people from all over Asia and beyond. Later, working with prospective German investors and Singapore Government agencies as an interpreter gave me an insight into the business world.

It has taken a while to get to know Singaporeans. The expat community seems to have a momentum all its own, and while everyone works in harmony, leisure time seems to be spent separately. But what a fascinating mix the people are!

Most of them are Chinese. Yet their ancestors came from so many different parts of China with such differences in dialect, cuisine and background that it's sometimes hard to think of them as one people. Nowadays most of them have never set foot in China and if asked, would say they were Singaporean by nationality.

Then there are the gentler Malays, no longer living their traditional *kampong* lives, but adapting to highrise flats and a much faster pace of life.

Indians, many of them with little knowledge of the Subcontinent make up the other major race, and are engaged in all kinds of enterprises here. Each race has its own distinct history, culture and religion.

Foreigners from all over the globe complete the mix, and we all learn about and from each other. Young Singaporeans are more of a mixture of cultures than their forebears. With a whole lot of western influence thrown in, values tend to merge and differences dissolve.

Singapore is Asia with all its charm, but with the advantage that the telephones work, the roads are spotless; and being so central, the rest of the region is on the doorstep.

The place changes fast, as buildings rise and disappear with alarming rapidity. Progress has led to much destruction, as efficiency has its price. But at last some parts of Singapore such as Chinatown and Tanjong Pagar are being preserved, and others like Bugis Street are being recreated as Singaporeans realise the value of their rich if short heritage.

Nowadays I live surrounded by colourful bougainvillaea, fragrant frangipani and African tulip trees laden with great vermilion flowers. But I'm just minutes away from the fashion houses of Europe, the arts of old China, the taste of India and some of the best hotels in the world. That's just part of the diversity that Singapore has to offer, and why I like living here.

Singapore is well geared to the tourist. There are so many tours, trips, maps and guidebooks that you may wonder why I have written yet another.

Well, most visitors tend to follow the beaten track of Orchard Road and the main streets of Chinatown, many thinking there's nothing else. So many see only a modern city with a slight Asian accent. But I'll take you down the side roads, behind the scenes, and show you some of Singapore's fascinating past and and equally interesting present and give you a glimpse of its peoples and their varied traditions.

Let me show you my Singapore, and you'll wish you were staying longer!

HISTOR

Singapore has grown from an outpost on the old East-West trade route to the busiest port in the world today, a city enjoying a reputation as a stable and efficient base for expansion in the South East Asian region.

It is tempting to view Singapore as the creation of two men, Sir Stamford Raffles, who founded the city in 1819, and Mr. Lee Kuan Yew, who as Prime Minister led it to prosperity after independence in 1965. Although a convenient simplification, the two names and dates are without doubt the most significant in the history of Singapore.

Not much is known about Singapore's distant past. Mere mentions in ancient Chinese texts precede the legendary changing of its name from that of Temasek, or "Sea Town", recorded in the *Malay Annals*.

The story goes that the Srivijayan ruler Sang Nila Utama, who had taken the title Sri Tri Buana, was on his way to explore the inviting sands of Temasek, when a storm almost overturned his ship. Throwing his crown into the sea, to lighten the load, he finally landed on the island. There he caught sight of a strange creature, with a red body, black head and white breast, which one of his party incorrectly identified as a lion, thus it acquired the name "Lion City" in Sanskrit – Singa Pura.

& Culture

Sri Tri Buana's settlement prospered due to its position on the trade route between China, Persia and Arabia. This aroused envy in the neighbours, and led to many invasion attempts, with Singapura eventually becoming part of the Javanese Majapahit Empire. After that, little is known until the early 19th century, by which time it was under the rule of the Sultan of Johor through his representative on the island, the Temenggong.

Shophouses along Boat Quay undergoing restoration

Modern Singapore began with the landing on January 28, 1819 of Sir Stamford Raffles, then Lieutenant-Governor of Bencoolen, who intended to establish a trading post for the East India Company to compete with Dutch dominance in the region. This he achieved by means of a treaty with the Sultan Hussein of Johor and the Temenggong signed on February 6, 1819.

His organisation of the settlement began, and despite frequent absences, when the Resident Colonel Farquhar was in charge, Raffles was ultimately responsible for the layout of the city. It was he who determined the location of the government sector, the European Town, areas for the Bugis, Arabs, Chulias and Malays. Chinatown was organised so that the Chinese of different classes and from different provinces lived in their own sections within the area to the southwest of the Singapore River. The construction of houses of masonry with tiled roofs, was also prescribed by Raffles, and we owe to him the shelter of the "five-foot way", or covered pavement.

Immigration, mainly of Chinese, many of them from Malacca, increased the population to 5,000 by June 1819. Trade flourished and the settlement grew in prosperity although slave trading thrived, as did opium smoking and prostitution.

The British took full possession in 1824, and in 1826 Singapore became part of the Straits Settlements. By 1832 it was the centre of government and then on April 1, 1867 the Straits Settlements became a Crown Colony. Singapore became an important port and coaling station on the route through the Suez Canal from Europe to the Far East. The rubber industry in Malaya began as a result of Henry Ridley's enthusiasm and work in Singapore's Botanic Gardens. Export was handled through Singapore, and the future looked secure.

The Japanese conquest on February 15, 1942 shattered the lives of colonials and locals alike, and nothing was ever the same again. For 3½ years, Singapore, renamed Syonan-to (Light of the South), was under Japanese rule, with the former overlords incarcerated. After the Japanese surrender in 1945, the British returned, and for several years attempted to retain their former hold on the colony. But times and attitudes had changed, and the British were never able to regain their former prestige after the humiliation of their quick defeat in 1942.

Independence was in the air, and after various attempts at compromise by the British with David Marshall and later Lim Yew Hock, against a background of insurrection led by the Communist Party of Malaya, Singapore finally attained self government on June 5, 1959. Lee Kuan Yew was sworn in as Prime Minister, having led his People's Action Party to victory in the first general election.

Merger with Malaya in a Federation of Malaysia with Sabah and Sarawak took place on September 16, 1963, to the displeasure of neighbouring Indonesia, which then began 3 years of armed confrontation.

But racial tensions and political differences soon led to a split with Kuala Lumpur, and on August 9, 1965 Singapore withdrew from the Federation and became a completely independent nation.

Lee Kuan Yew and his team then began nation building in earnest, coping with immediate basic problems facing the people of housing, unemployment and political unrest. During the late 1960s and in

Singapore's future

the 1970s they were able to turn their attention to building up the infrastructure, attracting foreign investment and moving Singapore into higher skilled industries, away from the cheap labour market towards developed nation status.

Political stability has been maintained through the 1980s and with an eye to the future the Old Guard leaders have made way for new blood.

On November 28, 1990, after 31 years as Prime Minister, Lee Kuan Yew handed over the reins of power to his chosen successor Goh Chok Tong and his team of second generation leaders. It was a smooth transition, the culmination of his policy of preparing Singapore for life without the "father of the nation", which ensured the continued stability and prosperity of the modern state he had led since independence.

Culture

The pattern of the island and the rhythm of the year spring from the inherent cultural diversity of Singapore. The immigrant peoples have given the place a melange of Malay, Chinese, Indian and European influences, all of which intermingle and are still evident behind the streamlined façade of the modern city.

Although nowadays citizens of all races tend to think of themselves as Singaporean, and live next to each other throughout the island, the areas designated for the different races by Sir Stamford Raffles still remain, each retaining its own particular atmosphere.

As you walk around the old streets of Chinatown, along Arab Street in the Muslim part of the city or stroll down Serangoon Road in Little India, you can appreciate the unique cultural background of each neighbourhood. All around the city are marks of the British colonial influence in the Neo-Classical buildings designed by George Coleman and enclaves of gracious black and white houses.

Each people has its own religion and all year round there are colourful festivals of special significance for different races, but enjoyed by all. Decorations go up and come down with remarkable speed. Some places have even been clever enough to use the same decorations for different festivals. One year, the Father Christmas' reindeers reappeared without their horns in February in celebration of the Chinese New Year of the Horse.

People

The original inhabitants of Singapore were Malay fishermen, and Malay is still the national language. Today Malays make up 15 percent of the population. Although few are able to maintain their traditional *kampong* (village) life here, as they have had to move into highrise flats, they have not changed their priorities. They are bound by the Islamic code, and for them family life is more important than material wealth. Many are involved in clerical work, the police force and in the communications industry. Although there are exceptions, on the whole theirs is a relaxed view of life, and they stand apart from the pressurised hothouse atmosphere of the commercial world.

That is where the Chinese thrive, and always have, from the earliest days of river trade to today's computerised stockmarket. They account for over 75 percent of the population, and are at the centre of the commercial and political spheres. Although stemming from regions all over China, each with its own culture and dialect, many Singaporean Chinese have lost touch with Mainland Chinese traditions. Dialects remain the *lingua franca* of the elderly, but all are encouraged to speak Mandarin, which is the medium of instruction in Chinese schools. Modern and sophisticated, The Chinese nevertheless prefer to keep on the right side of the gods of fortune, however nebulous. Many are still deeply influenced by age old tra-

ditions and beliefs. Spanking new offices are built and furnished in accordance with ancient *feng shui* (geomancy) principles. In 1971, this led to the doors of a hotel in Orchard Road being realigned at 32 degrees. Prosperity followed.

Indians, many originally convicts and indentured labourers, from South India, now make up 6½ percent of Singaporeans, and are well represented in politics and the law, as well as in journalism and commerce. Most are Hindus and they too carefully preserve their ancient customs and festivals.

The modern Chinese

Straits-born Chinese, or Peranakans, were the product of intermarriage with Malays. These *Baba*s and *Nonya*s (men and women) had their own culture and language, but all that remains now is their decorative architecture, colourful ceramics and delicious *nonya* cuisine.

Completing the mix of cultures is an expatriate community from all over the world, many staying only for a couple of years' contract, but others settling and making their home here.

Modern Singaporeans of different cultures mix and intermarry more than their predecessors did, and have an eye to the western world, as keen on rock music as their counterparts in the U.S.A. or Britain, although maintaining the Asian tradition of respect for age and family ties. On the whole, Singaporeans of today are fit, hardworking and proud of what their small island nation has achieved in its short life.

Religions

Religious tolerance is essential in Singapore, where adherents to the main faiths of the world live and worship cheek by jowl. Religions often cross the racial boundaries and some even merge in unusual ways in this cosmopolitan island.

Within Chinese temples, Taoism, Confucianism, Buddhism and ancestor worship blend in an eclectic mix. In the early days the Chinese would erect places of worship on arrival to thank the gods for their safe journey. These later became established temples.

Followers of "Tao", the Way, adhere to the teachings of the ancient Chinese sage Lao Tzu. They are concerned about the principles of astrology, and with the balance of the Yin and Yang, the opposite forces of heaven and earth, male and female. Here too is the origin of *feng shui*, which literally means wind and water, and according to which buildings are located, constructed and even furnished. Ancestor worship is common, and the spirits of the dead, like the gods themselves are appeased with offerings. One of the most popular deities is Kuan Yin, the Goddess of Mercy.

Most Buddhists are of the Mahayana school, although the Theravada school is also represented. But here the faith is linked with Taoism and the practical tenets of Confucianism.

Malays are Muslims, as are some Indians and Chinese. Islam has a fundamental influence in the lives of those who follow Mohammed, the Prophet of Allah, involving prayer five times a day, eating only *halal* food, which has been specially prepared in accordance with Islamic law, fasting during Ramadan and going to Mecca on the *Haj*.

With the arrival of Indian immigrants came Hinduism. The early temples are still the focal point of rituals and festivals held throughout the year.

Chinese wayang mural

Christian churches of all persuasions are to be found in Singapore, as missionaries arrived soon after Raffles, and people of all races are drawn to the faith.

There are two synagogues for the Jews and Sikhs, Zoroastrians and Jains are also represented.

Young Singaporeans tend to take what makes sense from the older generation and blend that with a more pragmatic world outlook. Many Chinese and Indians have become Christian, but the Malays remain true to Islam.

Many of Singapore's most interesting buildings are religious, whether old temples or modern churches or mosques, and an understanding of their meaning contributes to appreciation of their art.

Etiquette

What to visitors is a curiosity, to the believer is a matter of deep significance. If you remember that and act accordingly, you'll have no problems with etiquette in the temples of Singapore. Where there are strict rules, there are clear signs to advise you.

Chinese temples are relaxed and slightly chaotic. People pray, bowing with incense sticks clasped between their palms, buy and sell anything from "hell money" to paper umbrellas, and sit down to eat, all in and around the courtyard. Do remember to ask permission before taking photographs, particularly of elderly people.

In Hindu temples, devotees walk around freely and ceremonies are performed at certain times, often heralded with loud music. Shoes must be removed.

Ladies must be modestly dressed to enter a mosque, and may only enter certain areas. Again, shoes must be removed.

If you enter a Singaporean home, be prepared to take your shoes off and relax and enjoy yourself. Do, however, remember that Asians are more reticent than Westerners in discussing personal matters, and less inclined to public displays of affection.

HISTORY

1819: Sir Stamford Raffles sets up a trading post for the British East India Company with the agreement of the Sultan of Johor and the Temenggong, his representative on the island.

1824: The Sultan cedes Singapore in perpetuity to the British.

1826: Singapore, with Malacca and Penang, becomes part of the Straits Settlements, under the control of British India.

1867: The Colonial Office in London takes over control of Singapore.

1942: The Japanese, led by General Tomoyuki Yamashita, invade and occupy Singapore.

1945: The Japanese surrender and the Allied Forces return.

1946: Singapore becomes a Crown Colony.

1955: The Rendel Constitution granted by the British leads to elections and David Marshall becomes Chief Minister.

1956: Lim Yew Hock takes over as Chief Minister.

1958: A Constitutional Agreement for independence for Singapore is signed in London.

1959: The first General Election for a fully elected Legislative Assembly results in Lee Kuan Yew becoming Prime Minister as leader of the victorious People's Action Party (PAP).

1963: Singapore becomes part of the Federation of Malaysia.

1965: On separation from Malaysia, Singapore becomes an independent sovereign nation.

1967: Singapore issues its own currency.

1968: In the General Election the PAP win all 58 seats.

1981: In a by-election, Mr. J.B. Jeyaratnam of the Workers' Party wins the first seat to be held by an opposition member.
Singapore time is brought into line with Malaysian time, by putting the clocks forward by half an hour.

1988: Under a revised constitution the PAP win 80 seats in a General Election, with the Singapore Democratic Party winning one seat, and two members of the Workers' Party declared non-constituency MPs.

1990: Prime Minister Lee Kuan Yew hands over to Mr. Goh Chok Tong who forms the new government.

Here are two full day itineraries which will give you an introduction to Singapore, past and present. On the first day, my aim is to show you the heart of the city and to give you glimpses of history as we go along. On the second day we look at the lives and religions of the three main communities of Singapore.

As I've tried to pack a lot into these days, you might not feel like doing everything I've suggested; so choose whatever sounds interesting. These itineraries are just guidelines, so feel free to wander from the straight and narrow and explore any odd nooks and crannies on the way.

As it is hot and humid here all year round, it is better to take taxis for longer trips and save your energy for walking around the more interesting areas.

Remember to drink plenty of water to counteract dehydration, and to wear comfortable shoes and cool clothes. When it rains, it pours, especially in the wet season from November to February, so it's a good idea to take an umbrella with you. Local ladies preserve their fine skin by using umbrellas as parasols.

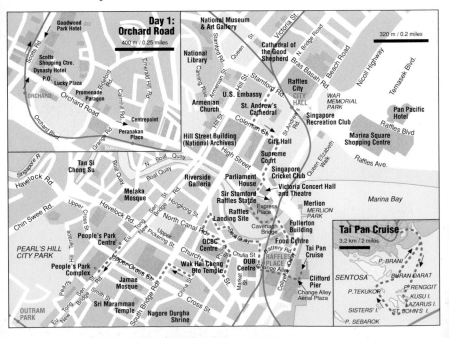

If you're thinking of visiting a mosque don't forget that strictly speaking, women should cover their knees and arms to go inside an Islamic place of worship, and then keep to the designated areas. Chinese and Indian temples have no such restrictions.

Now it's time to pick up the book and set off, at a leisurely Asian pace to discover Singapore!

Day 1

Getting Acquainted

St. Andrew's Cathedral and the Colonial heart of the city; The Singapore River, the business district and Collyer Quay. Lunch on an airconditioned Chinese-style vessel cruising around the harbour. A short afternoon walk in Chinatown, perhaps shopping in People's Park before going to Orchard Road for tea and a walk down to Peranakan Place for the evening.

St. Andrew's Catherdral and the Westin Stamford

Take the MRT to **City Hall** station and the exit for **St. Andrew's Cathedral**. Then walk through the peaceful churchyard into the cool interior of this lovely building. It was built by Indian convict labour using a plaster consisting of an extraordinary mixture of egg white, shell, lime, sugar, coconut husk and water known as Madras chunam.

Set in peaceful grounds, the present cathedral is the third place of worship to be built on this site. The first, in Palladian style, was designed by George Dromgold

Sport at the Padang

Coleman, the Irish architect who became Superintendent of Public Works and during the years 1828 to 1841 was responsible for the design of many of Singapore's loveliest buildings, including Parliament House, the Armenian Church and some of the elegant godowns or warehouses along the Singapore River.

His church was later altered by James Turnbull Thomson, who added a tower and steeple, but this was demolished in 1855 after twice being struck by lightning. The early English-Gothic style cathedral which now stands was designed by Lieutenant-Colonel Ronald MacPherson and consecrated in 1862.

A small leaflet giving the history and brief notes on the different parts of the cathedral can be found near the side entrance.

Leave the cathedral on the diagonal path leading southwards towards a green expanse known as **The Padang** (Malay for "field"). This area, formerly known as **The Esplanade**, has always been at the centre of life in Singapore. You'll often see prints of paintings by John Turnbull Thomson where Coleman's buildings, among them the early St. Andrew's, the Armenian Church and some spacious bungalows form the background to the colonial scene at "Scandal Point". This end of the Padang was no doubt thus named because it was the venue for evening outings to enjoy the slightly cooler air, a time and place to exchange the latest gossip.

With **The Singapore Cricket Club** at the end on the right, **The Recreation Club** on the left, this playing field in the heart of Singapore's colonial district has an interesting past.

The Rec' Club was built on the site of the *attap* (palm frond) dwelling of Major Farquhar, the first Resident and assistant to Raffles. It was originally a club for Eurasians. The lovely Victorian-style Cricket Club used to be exclusively for Europeans. Nowadays membership is open at both ends of this green, where all kinds of activities, from cricket and rugby

Financial hub of Singapore

rugby to National Day celebrations take place.

In 1942, on the day following the Japanese Occupation, the European civilians were herded onto the Padang before being marched more than 22 km (14 miles) to Changi, where they were imprisoned. Lord Louis

The Merlion

Mountbatten accepted the Japanese surrender on the steps of **City Hall** just along on the right, on September 12, 1945. Here too Lee Kuan Yew declared Singapore's independence from Britain in 1959.

Next door is the green-domed **Supreme Court**. Buildings seem to have been erected and pulled down in rapid succession in Singapore since the very early days. Here the original house by Coleman was remodelled and eventually demolished to enable the Hotel de l'Europe to be built. This was demolished in 1900 and the Grand Hotel de l'Europe was constructed. This in turn made way for the present Supreme Court building in 1936.

Cross Coleman Street and you'll come to a bronze statue of an elephant, a gift from the King of Siam. It stands in the gardens of the lovely white **Parliament House**, which apart from an extension along the river bank has survived as Coleman designed it, despite

Sir Stamford Raffles

many changes of function, from private house to Government offices and court.

Walk on down Parliament Lane past **Empress Place Building,** formerly housing government offices, now renovated and housing major exhibitions of Chinese dynasties. Ahead is a statue of Sir Stamford Raffles, on the site of his first landing on the island of Singapore on January 28, 1819.

Turn left along the **Singapore River**. This was once the hub of trade, crammed with bumboats, small boats, often with eyes painted on the front, which plied between the ships in the harbour and the godowns upriver. Now the water is calm and empty after a massive clean-up campaign by the Government, which relocated the boats and purified the water. Look at the fascinating contrast of tumbledown old shophouses towered over by the gleaming highrise bank buildings of the city.

On your left are some food stalls, and ahead of you is **Cavenagh Bridge.** Just outside the splendid green and white Empress Place Museum is something which looks rather like Singapore's answer to I.M. Pei's Louvre pyramid. It is in fact a time capsule sealed in 1990 with items commemorating Singapore's 25 years of independence, and is to be opened on its 50th anniversary in 2015.

Behind the Empress Place Museum, crowned by a distinctive clock tower, is the lovely white building of the **Victoria Memorial Hall**

and Theatre. In front of this building stands the original sculpture of Raffles by Thomas Woolner, the copy of which we saw by the river. **The Singapore Symphony Orchestra** regularly gives concerts here, so you might like to check the programme at the booking office within.

Now you have a choice of lunch with the locals at the stalls, perhaps preceded or followed by a visit to the museum, or a lunch cruise. The stall food at this popular riverside haunt costs an average of S$2 per portion and the range is vast, with all kinds of local dishes such as *nasi goreng* (fried rice), *kuay teow* (noodles) and for the adventurous, pig's tongue, blood or intestines!

Victoria Concert Hall and Theatre

A more exciting option is a **Harbour Cruise** on board the *Tai Pan*, a Chinese-style boat where a buffet of Chinese dim sum (tidbits) is served as you sail. For this relaxing lunch break, make your way over the river by crossing the oldest bridge to span the river, now reserved for pedes-

Cavenagh Bridge

trians. You will find yourself in the business district of Singapore amid the bustle of the commercial world. At the main road of **Collyer Quay**, turn right and follow signs to the overpass to **Clifford Pier**.

The cruise sets off at 12.30 p.m. so if you are early browse through the shops in Aerial Plaza, many of them relocated from the now demolished Change Alley. There's everything from electronics to embroidery.

Down the escalator you will find yourself in a large hall and right at the end is the *Tai Pan* ticket office, where for S$30 you will get your cruise ticket which entitles you to the buffet lunch with Chinese tea (beer is available on board too). So just board the exotic vessel and look back at Singapore's Wall Street as you drift away past the statue of the **Merlion**, half fish, half lion, which is the symbol of Singapore.

The **Fullerton Building** is all that remains of the old waterfront, where merchants used to watch their ships as goods were taken ashore by *tongkangs*, or lighters, and bumboats. Boys used to dive into the harbour waters for coins thrown down from the ships, until loss of life to sharks eventually ended the frolics.

So much has changed here. Reclaimed land, traversed by the **East Coast Parkway** has formed **Marina Bay.** Ships now berth further

Clifford Pier Jetty

west where great yellow cranes hoist the huge boxes at the computerised **Tanjong Pagar Container Port** and at four other terminals around the island. The godowns upriver are decaying slowly, although one has been converted into **The Warehouse** discotheque. The bumboats rocking gently in the water now usually work over in Pasir Panjang or are used to ferry tourists on river tours.

The *Tai Pan* sails out under the **Benjamin Sheares Bridge** to the **Eastern Anchorage** where as many as 300 ships from all over the world may be seen, a glimpse of what makes Singapore the world's busiest port.

The cruise takes just an hour and a half, so relax and listen to the interesting commentary as you sightsee sitting down. Sun lovers will enjoy the upper deck, while those who've had enough heat can watch the scene in airconditioned comfort below. You'll pass the Container Port, Sentosa Island and sail around the lovely Southern Islands of St. John's, Sisters', Lazarus, Renggit and Kusu.

On your return, cross over the Aerial Plaza again but instead of taking the escalator down to street level, go through the central glass doors on the other side and follow the signs to **Raffles Place**. Formerly known as Commercial Square, this was the hub of colonial life. Here banks rubbed shoulders with the department stores of Robinson's (where the ladies would meet for morning coffee) and John Little. Both stores still exist but are now to be found in Orchard Road. Raffles Place has totally changed. It is now a pedestrian precinct enveloped by great highrise commercial buildings. The most spectacular is the soaring, acute angled OUB Centre, designed by Kenzo Tange.

There is an MRT station here if you wish to return to Orchard Road, otherwise we'll take a walk through Chinatown.

Make your way across to the right-hand side of the square and

Raffles Place

Henry Moore's sculpture

go straight on down to the river, turning left along **Boat Quay**. This was once a muddy swamp, which was then designated as the main commercial area by Raffles. It was he who began the trend of changing Singapore's shape by levelling a hill to form what is now Raffles Place and using the earth to fill in Boat Quay.

This stretch of river then became the centre of trade, where cargo boats were loaded and unloaded by coolies. These Chinese immigrants, engaged by a *khetow* or agent, would arrive here and work to pay off their passage to the *kongsi* which is rather like a company or clan. They worked as labourers, living in bachelor quarters until they had saved enough money to bring their wives and children over from China. Street vendors abounded and food was often served by itinerant hawkers with the meals being eaten by customers squatting in the streets.

Shophouses and godowns for Chinese and European traders were built further along the river bank but many men lived on their boats, which were anchored cheek by jowl.

Look at the lovely but ageing façades of the old shophouses. Some are now being converted into offices by enterprising companies such as Saatchi and Saatchi, while further up is a little pub called Paddles. A new kind of life is evolving on the river bank.

Plunge into **Chinatown** down **Canton Street**. See how plants can grow in impossible places, listen to the caged birds competing with high-pitched Chinese songs on the radio and get a whiff of cooking smells. On Circular Road turn right, and pass noisy shops selling everything from knickers to necklaces, offices open to the pavement with typewriters clicking busily, and old men frowning over papers in dingy rooms.

The quieter side of Chinatown

At the corner coffee shop make a sharp left down Lorong Telok passing the rattan worker amid a display of baskets of all shapes and sizes piling up around him and hanging from the ceiling. Go left again onto North Canal Road where you will find Chinese housewives buying dried food of every description, from sharks' fins and birds' nests to sea cucumbers. Maybe you'd like some nuts, ginseng or Chinese tea to take home.

Cross over to the OCBC Centre where a figure sculpted by Henry

27

Moore reclines, and bear left until you reach Phillip Street where you will see the elaborately carved roof of the **Wak Hai Cheng Bio Temple**. Heavy doors with golden gods lead into its dark interior with intricately carved beams, where sunlight filters through smoke from the incense coils onto fruit-laden altars.

Before wending our way back to the Orchard Road area, you may like to walk on through Chinatown to **People's Park**. This shopping centre is full of all sorts of interesting things, especially for the seamstress; fabrics from denim to the finest silks are sold at the lowest prices in town. You will have to bargain hard though. To get there turn right at Church Street and left into Chulia Street which you follow through to Cross Street. Just wandering through these little streets is a fascinating experience as you look into dark shops selling all kinds of strange-looking goods. Turn right and carry straight on up over South Bridge Road then New Bridge Road. There you will find People's Park, both Centre and Complex, where you can browse for hours.

If this sounds too much of a good thing make your way from Wak Hai Cheng Bio Temple back left along Church Street to the MRT station in Raffles Place and take a ride over to the Orchard Station.

Cross **Orchard Road**, the Oxford Street of Singapore, and go through **Tangs** to the **Dynasty Hotel** (the highrise pagoda) next door. Both are the property of the Tang family. C.K. Tang arrived in Singapore in 1922 and was the first trader to recognise the future importance of Orchard Road, now of course the main shopping street in Singapore. Being Christian, the Chinese cemetery opposite this site did not bother him. His business in Chinese arts and crafts flourished and he built a pagoda roofed curio shop which has now given way to the highrise hotel and swish department store. But the family business continues to sell Chinese curios as well as almost anything else you can think of. Tangs is closed on Sundays, which

The Dynasty Hotel is a landmark on Orchard Road

Goodwood Park Hotel lights up

is very unusual in Singapore, as the Tangs are still Christians and observe the day of rest.

In the Dynasty Hotel lobby are wonderful teak carved panels depicting Chinese history and legends. A booklet which you may read there, or buy for S$10, will tell you all about these glorious examples of traditional craftsmanship.

Perhaps you would like a drink in **Stroller's Sidewalk Cafe** right here or have tea at the **Goodwood Park Hotel**. Just along Scotts Road, this hotel with its distinctive tower was the Teutonia Club before World War I. Now it serves a traditional English tea, albeit buffet style, and you can choose from a wide selection of different teas, sandwiches, scones and cakes. Light, soothing music is played for you as you relax and recover from the rigours of sightseeing.

Thus fortified, you can retrace your footsteps to Orchard Road via **Scotts Shopping Centre**, which has an excellent range of silks and garments at the China Silk House and other good clothes shops to tempt you.

Then simply shop your way down Orchard Road, through Lucky Plaza, the Promenade, the Paragon and just after Esprit, you'll find

Restoration work began on Peranakan Place in 1984

one remaining row of little shops which is how Orchard Road used to be. By the time you reach the lovely old pastel houses of **Peranakan Place** in Emerald Hill Road, you'll know the meaning of our adage, that in Singapore you can shop until you drop. The history of this lovely street is given in the Mixed Heritage itinerary.

Drop in at **Apa Villa**, No. 23, which has an art gallery featuring the best of local and foreign works.

Happy Hour at **Bibi's the Pub** is from 4 to 8 p.m., if you need a drink. Otherwise, simply flop down in Emerald Mall for a while, for there are lots more shops yet!

Robinson's is now just next door at **Centrepoint,** along with an enormous selection of other shops, including Marks and Spencer and The Body Shop. In **Cuppage Road**, just around the corner are galleries and shops selling wares from all over Asia. If you go upstairs you'll find the **Della Butcher Gallery**, where local artists hold exhibitions, and there's always a selection of recent work on show.

Everything stays open late so you can explore this part of town until the evening. You can then dine alfresco in one of the street cafes or explore Emerald Hill Road. In **Aziza's** you can taste Malay food in a cosy *kampong*-like setting. You'll also find **Casablanca**, a Peranakan house transformed into a wine bar and restaurant on the theme of the film. If you feel like a good continental dinner, the cuisine is excellent, but as it's a popular place it's a good idea to reserve a table.

For nightbirds, **The Saxophone** in Cuppage Road is the in-place for live jazz. There, you can sit out under the stars at the end of your first day in Singapore and just watch the world go by.

Emerald Mall Cafe

Day (2)

Temples and Tempting Traditional Crafts

Start off at a local market, then enjoy an Indian breakfast before a stroll around a Hindu temple and two very different Chinese temples. Lunch with a breathtaking view right over Singapore as far as Malaysia and Indonesia. Spend the afternoon browsing in Arab Street where you will visit a mosque, and on to "Thieves' Market" in Sungei Road. Evening at the Satay Club and Marina Square.

Today you'll visit places of worship of the three main communities of Singapore, Indian, Chinese and Malay. You will see a fascinating Hindu temple, followed by two very different Chinese temples which combine Buddhism and Taoism (with a little ancestor worship thrown in), and during the afternoon a Malay mosque where Allah is worshipped. Along the way we'll browse through shops selling traditional wares and see how the people live and work.

Although parts of Singapore are predominantly the domain of one or other of the main racial groups, such as Little India, Chinatown and the Malay area of Kampong Glam, all over the island the races mingle, living and worshipping in different ways, in close proximity and in harmony. This morning, to avoid hopping all over town, we'll visit Indian and Chinese temples in Little India. The area is described in greater detail in the Little India itinerary, so it's a good idea to read that section, then choose how much you want to see.

As we are planning to visit a mosque, and our lunchtime venue has a smart casual dress code of no jeans, shorts or collarless T-shirts, please dress appropriately.

We begin before breakfast by taking a taxi to **Serangoon Road,** to what is locally known as K.K. or **Kandang Kerbau Market**, meaning "Buffalo Pen" in Malay. In the old days this was indeed a cattle market. It is still the site of a fascinating "wet" market selling live chickens and all kinds of meat and fish. There are myriads of colourful stalls where you'll find exotic fruit

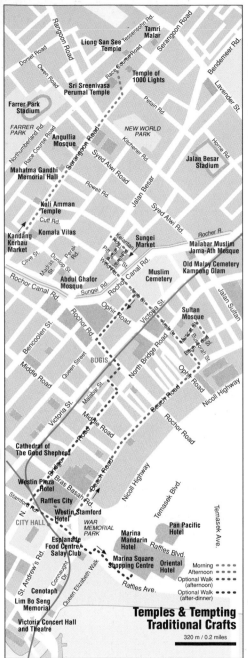

Temples & Tempting Traditional Crafts

320 m / 0.2 miles

Morning -----
Afternoon -----
Optional Walk -----
(afternoon)
Optional Walk -----
(after-dinner)

and vegetables. Women of all nationalities come here to buy spices and foodstuffs for every type of Asian cuisine.

The official name of the building, rarely heard, is the Zhu Jiao Centre. Later in the day a variety of stalls upstairs open for business.

Wherever you go in Singapore you'll find people eating, and in this market foodstalls reflect the cosmopolitan atmosphere.

Cross Serangoon Road and you'll feel as if you have been transported to Delhi. Pungent spices assail your nostrils, loud music and car horns blast in your ears and a riot of colour surrounds you.

Many of the women are resplendent in brightly coloured *sari*s, while the men are comfortable in the traditional Indian *dhoti* or local *sarong* (literally "tube" in Malay) a piece of coloured or check-patterned cloth wrapped around the waist. Trishaws wobble in and out of the traffic delivering piles of washing and provisions or taking people to work. Watch the garland maker entwine colourful blooms and inhale the scent of jasmine.

You might like to explore the Indian supermarket of **P. Govindasamy Pillai**. Downstairs you'll find flour, rice, spices, utensils and everything you could ever need for Indian cooking. Upstairs is a treasure trove of Indian silks, sold in *sari* lengths of 5½ metres (18 ft), and costing from S$30 to well over S$500 for exquisite cloth embroidered with gold thread.

Further along , at a tiny roadside stall a vendor is making *pan*, by wrapping up areca nut, gambier, tobac-

Indian Fortune-teller

co and a little lime in *serai* (betelnut leaf). This mixture costing 10 cents is chewed by Indians and Malays, and supposedly aids digestion and promotes potency.

Don't miss having your fortune told by the green parakeet, who will pick out a card for S$1.

Then go into the airconditioned cool of **Komala Vilas**, noisy and full downstairs but calmer upstairs. It's time to savour a crispy 50-cm long *Dosa* or pancake, which makes the most delicious breakfast, for just S$1.40. Local coffee sweetened with condensed milk is the usual accompaniment.

As you leave, turn right and walk on up the road, or take a taxi or bus up to **Sri Sreenivasa Perumal Temple,** about a 20-minute walk away. On the left you pass the ornately carved and brightly coloured entrance or *gopuram* of the **Sri Veerakaliamman Temple.** There Kali, the consort of Shiva, one of the three main Hindu deities, is worshipped. This temple is discussed in detail in the Little India itinerary.

As you walk on up Serangoon Road, you will see Muslims praying at the **Angullia Mosque**. This mosque was built over 100 years ago, but has since been renovated.

Further on you come to another wonderful *gopuram*, rising to a height of over 21 metres (70 ft). This is the entrance to the **Sri Sreenivasa Perumal Temple**. This bright and elaborately decorated temple, founded in the mid 19th century, was almost completely rebuilt in the 1960s by craftsmen from South India. P. Govindasamy Pillai was the benefactor responsible for this and the enormous *gopuram* which was built 10 years later. Remember the shop bearing his name at the end of Serangoon Road? It is now run by his sons.

The figures on the *gopuram* depict the various incarnations of Vishnu, also known as Perumal, the Preserver of Life, who appears on earth from time to time in different avatars and to whom the temple is dedicated.

You might be lucky enough to hear the beating of drums heralding a procession of devotees led by the priest, followed by women with flowers in their hair, carrying offerings.

It is from here that the annual Thaipusam procession begins in February. Devotees who have prepared themselves by fasting are said to lose no blood as they pierce their tongues, cheeks and skin with spikes and skewers, to support great arched structures made of steel and decorated

with peacock feathers, called *kavadis*. They then walk all the way to the Chettiar Temple in Tank Road where they deposit the *kavadis*. This is done either as an act of penance or gratitude to Lord Murugan, Shiva's son. The great procession is an awesome sight on this day.

In the **Sri Sivan Temple** next door you may see worshippers walking round and round nine dark stone carved figures representing the nine planets of the Hindu universe. They stop before the one corresponding to the day of their birth.

Leave the temple and to your left you will see a path through an HDB (Housing Development Board) estate. These flats are typical of the low cost housing provided by the Singapore government, in which 87 percent of the population now live. Washing flutters on poles suspended from the windows while plants, caged birds and lanterns brighten up the scene.

Out on Race Course Road, turn right, and you will come to the Chinese **Temple of 1000 Lights**, so called because the 15-metre (50 ft) high statue of the Buddha is surrounded by light bulbs. Just inside the door is part of a branch of the sacred Bodhi tree under which the Buddha attained enlightenment. There is also an enlargement of the Buddha's footprint, inlaid with mother of pearl.

All around the base of the great figure are windows where colourful figures depict scenes from the life of Prince Siddharta. Follow the story round and enter the little room at the back where a figure of a reclining Buddha shows how he passed away from the earth.

Over the road are some lovely old houses and the Taoist **Liong San See Temple** with its womderfully carved roof.

The temple is dedicated to Kuan Yin, the Goddess of Mercy,

The Buddha in the Temple of 1000 lights

who has eighteen arms to help all those in distress. Seated in front of her is the Buddha. Kuan Yin is a popular deity and you will see people bowing repeatedly in prayer, holding incense sticks between the palms of their hands.

The temple is peaceful, a haven of red and gold glowing in the flickering candle-light. The altar table is laden with fruit, and the air heavy with incense. Above are intricately carved wooden beams.

If you go through to the courtyard at the back, you will see hundreds of memorial tablets. There relatives of the deceased pray for the souls of the departed.

Back out in the fresh air, hail a taxi to **Raffles City** for a look at Singapore from above. At the **Westin Stamford Hotel** you take the special lift up to **The Compass Rose Restaurant**. As you leave the high speed lift, with your ears still popping, you will gaze right across Singapore to Malaysia, and as you walk around you can read the island like a map down below. To the south are the ships and in the distance the islands of Indonesia.

After a refreshing drink, savour the delights of the seafood buffet (S$39.00++) while enjoying the spectacular view. For a souvenir ask for the letter-form printed with a panorama indicating the main landmarks (and with some tempting cocktail ideas on the back).

Make the most of this lunch break before hailing a cab along Beach Road, which as its name suggests, was once the seashore. Stop at the corner of **Arab Street**, the Islamic area of Singapore. The history of this area, designated for Arabs and Malays by Raffles, is described in more detail in the Kampong Glam itinerary.

The World's Tallest Hotel

Arab Street is full of traditional Islamic and Malay wares, such as prayer mats, black caps called *songkok*s, lace caps for *Haji*s and *Haja*s (men and women who have made the pilgrimage to Mecca), copies of the Koran and even tambourines used in wedding ceremonies.

But that's not all. It's a colourful cornucopia of batik, bangles, baubles, buttons, beads and baskets ... big baskets, little baskets, baskets hanging from the rafters and baskets all over the pavement.

Temptations abound with brilliant floral *sarong* lengths, wraparound skirts, patterned shirts, shoes, hats, mats and jewellery.

Go along Baghdad Street for shops chock-a-block with leather bags and shoes and turn left at Bussorah Street for a perfect view of the golden-domed **Sultan Mosque** framed by delightful shophouses. You might hear the muezzin calling the faithful to prayer from the minaret. Go up into the mosque, which is spacious and quiet.

As you leave, turn right and carry on browsing along Arab Street until you come to Rochor Canal Road, from where you cross over the canal to Sungei Road and the lively jumble of **Thieves' Market** where vendors spread their wares all over the street. If you look hard enough you can find anything from wellingtons to watches (the cheapest fakes in town) and if you really delve into the junk you might just discover an antique.

Then go back over the canal and down Arab Street, turning right into Queen Street to Rochor Road. Ahead of you is an area which will eventually be a recreation of Singapore's notorious **Bugis Street**, loved by the visitors, demolished by the government, and soon to return, cleaner but not duller, one hopes.

The next stop is City Hall, either on the MRT from Bugis Station, by taxi or on foot. Walkers make your way down Malabar Street and Bugis Street then turn right into North Bridge Road which will lead you to the back of the high Raffles City Tower, where you had lunch.

Over towards the sea, across Connaught Drive is the **Satay Club**, open air stalls selling succulent pieces of meat barbequed on bamboo skewers. This is a great place for alfresco dining right in the heart of old Singapore.

If you fancy a touch of the new, explore **Marina Square** where three hotels, **The Oriental, The Marina Mandarin and The Pan Pacific**, each with a spacious atrium and linked by a shopping complex, were designed by the American John Portman and Associates on reclaimed land. The bubble lift creeping up the outside of the Pan Pacific Hotel offers the visitor with a strong stomach a glorious, expanding view of the harbour and city as you rise up from the pool of water below. The **Hai Tien Lo Chinese Restaurant** at the top offers a more relaxed way of appreciating the scenery if you prefer dinner up high.

These hotels have nightclubs and discos, so there's no need to go home too early!

Shopping in Little India. Right, a
Thaipusam procession

Pick & Choose

A.M. Itineraries

1. Chinatown

A walk through old Chinatown, looking at temples and shophouses to recently renovated Tanjong Pagar.

Let's start in the heart of old Singapore, where trade began in *attap* huts, flourished in narrow shophouses and continues today in gleaming highrises.

Take a taxi to the oldest Chinese temple in Singapore, the **Thian Hock Keng Temple** (Temple of Heavenly Bliss) in **Telok Ayer Street.** Before land reclamation in the 1880s, this was the seashore, and it was here that newly-arrived immigrants erected a joss house to give thanks to Ma-Zu-Po, the Goddess of the Sea. Inside the temple, her statue, imported in 1840 from Amoy in China still stands, between the God of Prosperity and the God of Health. This temple was completed in 1842 by craftsmen using materials from China, and without using a single nail.

Dragons, for the Chinese, are divine creatures, not the symbol of evil they are in the west and here they chase the central

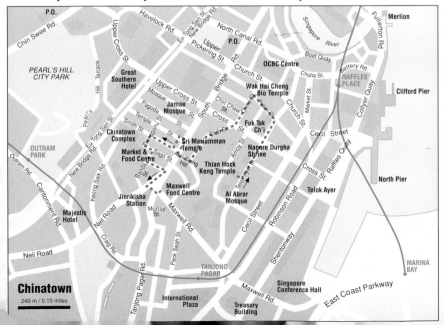

Chinatown just before the Lunar New Year

flame of immortality on the roof of the temple and wind their way around solid granite columns. Buddhists and Taoists worship here, and the temple is suffused with incense and the altars piled with offerings of fruit. Door gods and stone lions guard the entrance.

Telok Ayer Street was once the most important street in Singapore, as evidenced by the many religious buildings and clan associations which formed a nexus for the early immigrant community.

Turn left outside the temple, and look up to see the juxtaposition of old and new which typifies Singapore. High above the old shop houses the city buildings rise into the sky, in the streets rickety trishaws are peddled amid shining Mercedes cars, and on the pavements neat office girls sashay pass bent, old women pushing carts loaded with oddments to sell.

Turn left and walk pass a tiny green oasis to the **Nagore Durgha Shrine**, also known as the Masjid Chulia (mosque). Read the plaque on the wall, and then peep in. The outside is interesting, as classical columns support the Indian influenced upper storey.

Continue up Telok Ayer Street, over Cross Street and have a look at the **Fuk Tak Chi Temple**. Just after that you'll find a shop selling candles, incense and "hell money" and all kinds of paper articles, phones and even mansions which are burned to send to the deceased for his "journey west". Turn left into **Pekin Street,** and then left again into **China Street,** past shops selling all kinds of

dried foods, cakes and fish. Most interesting of all is the Chinese Medical Hall along on the left, where all kinds of esoteric medicines are sold, anything from pearls (which the pharmacist will grind to a powder) to dried birds' nests, snakes and seahorses which are boiled for several hours, the

39

Gaily decorated to catch the eye

resulting soup being beneficial.

At Chin Chew Street, cross the road to the jewellers, where Chinese gold (22K and 24K) can be traded in for new designs.

Up on the right is a shop selling "hell money", "passports" and lovely brass incense burners. In the last shop you can see noodles and *popiah* skins for making spring rolls being made.

Go over Cross Street into Club Street, perhaps taking a few moments to rummage through the first shop on the left. On the next corner wooden images of Chinese gods are carved.

Then walk right on through Club Street, past the barber in the five-foot way and cross to the right side to look at the pretty façade of No. 40. As you stand under the front door, look up at the peephole, through which the residents above observe the prospective visitor below.

As the road bends right into Ann Siang Hill you'll pass dark

shops, some making dragon heads, some cars for the next world, just keep your eyes open for interesting things.

When you reach South Bridge Road, cross over, turn to your right. You'll see the twin towers of the **Jamae Mosque**, rather like the Nagore Durgha

Sizzling barbequed pork slices, anyone?

Shrine and the ornamental *gopuram* over the entrance to the **Sri Mariamman Temple**, the oldest Hindu Temple in Singapore. It started life as a wooden building in 1827 on this site, chosen for its proximity to water, necessary for performing the rites. The most important annual festival is that of Thimithi, a fire-walking ceremony held in July or August in honour of the Goddess Draupadi.

Turn right as you leave the temple, into Temple Street, and wander down to Trengganu Street, where you can examine exotic Chinese products displayed outside two shops there.

If you'd like to see the "wet" market, Chinatown Centre, a modern building, is just on down at the corner of Sago Street. In the basement vegetables and live snakes, frogs and turtles are sold (not as pets but for the pot).

Behind there is Sago Lane, once known as the Street of the Dead for its death houses, where the old and chronically sick would wait out their time.

Then go on down Banda Street and you will emerge in South Bridge Road again. Turn right and cross over to Neil Road. Now you are in the conservation area of Tanjong Pagar, a fascinating place to explore. You'll find everything from English pubs to relocated clog makers.

On the corner is the renovated Jinrikisha Station, once the centre for these man-pulled conveyances, now a seafood restaurant. Just across Tanjong Pagar Road is Maxwell Road, where you'll find Food Alley, a road of different restaurants serving all kinds of Asian food.

But first, maybe your feet are killing you, and you'd like a cup of tea. So find the **Tea Chapter** at 9A, take off your shoes, go upstairs and let yourself be served Chinese tea in traditional style.

If you like, spend the afternoon exploring this part of Chinatown which has been so beautifully revitalised.

2. Little India

An experience of the Subcontinent as you walk around the Serangoon Road area known as "Little India".

You might like a light breakfast before this walk, as we take about half an hour to reach the coffeeshop. Ask the taxi driver to take you to the corner of **Serangoon Road** and Rochor Canal Road where you'll see a carpark on the right.

This area, never officially designated for Indians, simply attracted them in the early years of this century because it was the centre of the brick and cattle industry. Indians, both free and convict labour, were responsible for some of Singapore's most lovely buildings, including St. Andrew's Cathedral. Although there are no longer any kilns or cattle, "Little India" remains alive with noise, colour and exotic aromas and is still the heart of the Indian community.

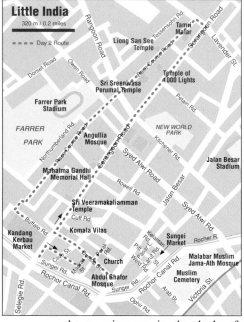

Little India

320 m / 0.2 miles

Day 2 Route

Rangoon Road
Tessensohn Rd.
Serangoon Road
Lavender St.
Tamil Matar
Liong San See Temple
Race Course Road
Dorset Road
Owen Road
Temple of 1000 Lights
Sri Sreenivasa Perumal Temple
Petain Rd.
Farrer Park Stadium
FARRER PARK
Northumberland Rd.
Race Course Road
Serangoon Road
NEW WORLD PARK
Kitchener Rd.
Angullia Mosque
Syed Alwi Road
Jalan Besar Stadium
Mahatma Gandhi Memorial Hall
Rowell Rd.
Jalan Besar
Syed Alwi Rd.
Sri Veeramakaliamman Temple
Cuff Rd.
Komala Vilas
Kandang Kerbau Market
Buffalo Rd.
Kelantan Rd.
Sungei Market
Rocher R.
Clive St.
Dunlop St.
Pitt St.
Pasar Rd.
Weld Rd.
Rochor Canal Rd.
Malabar Muslim Jama-Ath Mosque
Sungei Rd.
Church
Mayo St.
Madras St.
Abdul Ghafor Mosque
Sungei Rd.
Muslim Cemetery
Selegie Rd.
Rochor Canal Rd.
Ophir Rd.
Arab St.
Victoria St.

Just like the Subcontinent itself, "Little India" is an attack on the senses. Take a look up Serangoon Road – see the bustle of bright silk *saris*, the *dhoti*-clad men, the multi-coloured flowers of the garland-maker, the gold jewellery glittering in the windows and bikes and trishaws winding in and out of the stream of cars. Listen to vendors shouting, trishaw bells, car horns, brakes screeching and radios blaring out different Indian songs from all directions.

Inhale the pungent aroma of cooking curries and sharp spices as you refuse the trishaws eager for business on the corner. Feel the cool shelter from the morning sun in the shade of the arched five-foot way along **Hastings Road.**

Here the shops spill out onto the street and you are surrounded by exotic spices and vivid merchandise. Aromatic powders of all colours from bright yellow turmeric to deep red chilli are piled high in sacks. Boxes spill over with cloves, sticks of cinnamon, nutmegs, green cardamom pods, black peppercorns and seeds of coriander, cumin, fennel and mustard. Outside are baskets full of onions, garlic, dried chillies and dried fish and prawns of all shapes and sizes. Poppadoms, pulses, rice, ghee, saffron and even asafetida, anything you'll ever need to cook an Indian meal can be found in these packed provision stores.

Colourful garlands on sale in Little India

Either continue straight along Dalhousie Lane (named after the Marquis of Dalhousie, Governor General of India from 1848 to 1856) or meander through Clive Street and Campbell Lane to **Madras Street.** Here the houses have bright façades with coloured tiles and lacy tracery. Look out for mirrors above the doors which deflect evil, believed to travel in a straight line.

At the end of Madras Street is Dunlop Street. Turn right and walk on until you reach the blue gates of the **Abdul Ghafor Mosque**. You'll enter an oasis of tranquility, a little courtyard shaded by a fruit-laden mango tree. Steps lead up to the star-studded mosque with its gracefully curved arches and windows. In the houses opposite, surmounted with the star and crescent, Muslims both Indian and Malay quietly carry on with their lives while prayers and Islamic instruction take place inside the mosque.

Now it's time to join the locals for breakfast. Retrace your steps down Dunlop Street, and turn right into Perak Road. Join the schoolchildren and taxi drivers in the corner coffee shop. Not much English is spoken, but enough to understand your order.

On the far side, a dour Indian slaps, pounds, stretches and folds wheat flour dough before tossing it onto a black, round griddle. This delicious Indian bread, served with a separate dish of curry sauce is *roti prata*. At just 40 cents it is the best value in town.

The Chinese menu is good too though. Watch the lady with her chopsticks dunking noodles of all shapes and sizes into a cauldron of boiling broth and expertly retrieving them to serve with prawns and vegetables.

Order coffee, which will come sweet and laced with condensed milk unless you like it black and

Making *Prata* in a small coffeeshop

order *kopi-o*. Enjoy these local
treats and then sit awhile and
watch the backstreet life of
"Little India".

Wander on down Dunlop
Street towards Serangoon Road,
past **V.P. Mutton**, one of the last
of the butcher's shops left here.
Go on past displays of bright Indian cottons to the cool haven of
tasteful arts and crafts offered in **Chella's Gallery.** She has the best
selection of Indian *papier mâché* in town and all kinds of artefacts
and furniture. Walk on past little roadside tailors' shops and look
at the *mamak* ("uncle" in Tamil) man's wares displayed in the wall
cupboard shop. He sells everything from tea to toothpaste, all packed
onto shallow shelves set in the house wall.

Back on Serangoon Road again, browse through the shops which
you may have seen if you followed the Day 2 itinerary. You'll see
jewellers where ornate 22K earrings, necklaces, bracelets and anklets
sparkle and where you'll sometimes find parts of the body or cobras
crafted in silver, for use in supplication at the temple.

Pictures of Mrs. Gandhi, Jesus, Indian deities and film stars adorn
walls and a green parakeet waits to pick out the card telling your
fortune for S$1. Flour and spices are ground in the old fashioned
way at **Ramasamy Flourmill**.

Over the road is **Handlooms,** a treasure trove of Indian soft furnishings, clothes and carvings, sponsored by the Indian Government.

Further along is the **Sri Veeramakaliamman Temple**. This Hindu
temple is dedicated to Kali, consort to Shiva. Both deities are feared
as well as loved, for they represent the elemental powers of the universe. Shiva's consort is known as Parvati in her benign form but

Hindu devotees in prayer

Sri Veeramakaliamman Temple

as Kali she is powerful and destructive, the manifestation of anger against evil. Her black statue is at the centre of the temple.

To the left of the temple, Kali is shown with her two sons, Ganesh, the elephant god and Murugan, the child god, who is sometimes depicted with four heads. At the back is the gory figure of Kali disembowleling her hapless victim.

In the right hand corner of the hall are nine stones arranged in a square, representing the nine planets in the Hindu universe. Devotees circle this three times and stop in front of the planet day on which they were born.

If you followed the Day 2 Itinerary, you may now prefer to explore this fascinating area on your own before making your way through to Race Course Road later for lunch.

Otherwise, carry on up the road, just making a brief foray up Race Course Lane to take a look at a bust of Mahatma Gandhi in the **Gandhi Memorial Hall**, the foundation stone of which was laid by Jawaharlal Nehru in 1950.

Then follow the Day 2 walk on up the road to the brightly coloured *gopuram* over the entrance to the **Sri Sreenivasa Perumal Temple**, and read all about it.

Instead of going straight through to Race Course Road, continue up Serangoon Road to look at the **Sri Vadapathira Kaliamman Temple.** It is closed between noon and 4 p.m. though, so don't leave it too late to explore another fascinating Hindu temple, dedicated to Kali.

If, with the poet William Blake, you feel that
"A robin redbreast in a cage,

Liong San See Temple

Puts all Heaven in a rage."

then Wee's Pets, opposite, is not the place for you. Hundreds of local birds sing sadly and hop unhappily around their cages, waiting for buyers. Their prices range from S$20 to over S$1000 for a cockatoo. Keeping songbirds is a traditional pastime here, and owners gather in cafes to let their birds sing together and often compete. One such cafe, alive with birdsong in the mornings, is at the corner of Tiong Bahru and Seng Poh Roads, and at The Jurong Bird Park you can breakfast with the birds.

At Balestier Road, turn left and sample crisp banana or sweet potato fritters at 25 cents each from the coffeeshop there as you walk on taking a left turn into **Race Course Road.**

Just along on the right is the small Chinese temple of **Beo San Hood Chor** where Kuan Yin, the Goddess of Mercy is worshipped amid red candles and incense sticks smoking in brass containers. The atmosphere is relaxed and homely. If you peep round the back you may see old ladies relaxing in front of the T.V.

Just along on the right is the ornately decorated 80-year-old Chinese **Liong San See Temple**, which is described in the Day 2 itinerary as is the **Temple of 1000 Lights** across the road.

Walk on down past flats on the right which have the modern day equivalent of the five-foot way. Raffles' idea seems to have been extremely practical and long lasting.

You may be wondering why there is no race course. Well, there used to be one just behind the lowrise estate on the right where Farrer Park is today. Apart from being the venue for horse racing, this green expanse was where the first plane landed in 1911 and in 1919 the first flight from England to Australia made a stop here. Carry on down, past the Foochow Methodist

Way to heaven on the Temple of 1000 lights

Church to Rotan Lane. There in front of you is a row of the best Indian restaurants in Singapore, and after all that walking you'll be ready for a hot curry, eaten from a banana leaf (with your fingers) and an ice-cold beer.

After lunch you might like to make your way over to K.K. Market and explore the upstairs

Grab a trishaw to Kandang Kerbau Market

stalls, where apart from clothing of all kinds you will also find a fascinating collection of brass and antiques. There's much to see before your visit to this offshoot of India draws to a close.

3. Of Bird and Beasts

A day out in Jurong at the Bird Park and the Crocodile Paradise.

Make an early start to avoid the crowds and see the birds being fed at the **Jurong Bird Park**. If you take a taxi at about half past eight in the morning, you'll arrive when the park opens at 9 a.m., and the fare will be about S$15. The entrance fee is S$6 plus S$1 for the tram ride.

The Bird Park is spread over 20 hectares (49½ acres) of lush hillside, with some 4,500 birds of almost 420 species from all over the world. As you arrive you will hear the calls of the birds and see many non-residents flying above.

Pretty flamingoes

The Bird Park is busy renovating at the moment, so some of the exhibits are in spanking new premises. One of these, and the first you come to, is the **Penguin Parade**. You get a clear view of just how these unusual birds seem to fly under water.

Walk slowly over to the **Songbird Terrace** and enjoy the lakeside buffet to the trilling of the China Thrush, the White-rumped Shama, the Red-whiskered Bulbul and the Magpie-Robin as you breakfast with the birds.

The **Fuji World of Hawks** show is at 10 a.m. over at the Fuji Hawk Centre. It features eagles, falcons, owls and the magnificent condor. Afterwards you might like to look at the Falconry Museum.

There are other fascinating bird shows throughout the morning. There's **Hornbill Chit Chat** at 11 a.m. over at the Hornbill Exhibit and a multi-media show at the Nature Theatrette at 11.30 a.m., with an audio-visual show at noon. Check the show times and plan your route accordingly.

The stunning **Hornbill and Toucan Exhibit** is where these extraordinary, wonderfully coloured, noisy great birds have their perches high up in the trees. The whole park is packed with birds from every corner of the globe, so take your time to enjoy a close look at these exotic creatures.

After you have wandered around the striking array of exhibits, enter the **World of Darkness** to catch a rare glimpse of nocturnal birds.

Of Birds and Man

Around lunchtime leave the Bird Park and cross the carpark to the **Crocodile Paradise**. You can have lunch there in the Seafood Paradise, and even try crocodile meat.

The energetic might like to take an afternoon walk up the road behind the Bird Park for lunch in the Hilltop Restaurant, where you have a wide choice of Indonesian, Japanese or Western cuisine, and a fascinating view of the Jurong port and the southern islands. Up on this hilltop is a beautiful park with trees planted by famous (some are now infamous) visitors to Singapore.

After lunch, go into the Crocodile Paradise for S$4.50 and take the tram right round to look at the Crocodilian Enclosure, never mind the smell. Then visit the **Cavern of Darkness** and the **Underwater Viewing Gallery**. Wander around the gardens, looking at the piles of muddy-coloured pythons in their cage and in solitary splendour, two golden pythons curled around the branches of their enclosure.

Let the lovely Japanese *koi* fish tickle your fingers as you feed them. They have no teeth so don't be afraid. In fact they might be the frightened ones as they are extremely good eating, and a highly expensive delicacy.

You can shop until 3 p.m. when it's show time with upbeat music and great crocodiles being heaved out of the water to be danced with and kissed!

After that take bus 251, 253 or 255 to Jurong Interchange, which is right by the MRT station. There is also a feeder service to Orchard Road from the Bird Park which leaves at 3.45 p.m. and 5.15 p.m. and cost S$5, as well as plenty of taxis.

However, while you are on the western side of the island you could go on over to the Haw Par Villa (see A.M. Itinerary 8), which is along Pasir Panjang Road.

4. Of Flora and Fauna

Go and see a hillside covered with thousands of brightly-coloured orchids, then visit one of the most beautiful zoos in the world.

An early start by taxi to the **Mandai Orchid Gardens** in the north of the island will cost about S$15. Ask the driver to take you via Upper Thomson Road, and you will drive through some of Singapore's peaceful but fast-disappearing rural countryside.

Admission to the garden is S$1.50. Enjoy the exotic blooms growing in the sunshine on a gentle slope and see how orchids are grown. Then walk down to the peaceful Water Garden.

One of the most wonderful souvenirs you can buy in Singapore is a box of orchids, as with proper care the flowers will last for many weeks. You can buy a selection chosen for you at S$15 for a dozen sprays, or choose your own. If you don't want to carry a box around now, you can buy some at the airport when you leave.

After that, walk along the road to the right (for about 15 minutes), or take a bus to the **Singapore Zoological Gardens**. Bordering Seletar Reservoir, in a glorious setting of secondary forest, the zoo covers 90 hectares (22 acres), 28 of which have been developed for exhibits. Admission is just S$5.

The zoo is often called "The Open Zoo" as most of the animals are cleverly separated from people by water moats and other concealed or low-profile barriers to ensure an unobstructed view. Mostly from around South East Asia, you can see them in enclosures very like their natural habitat.

Different species which cohabit happily in the wild are also displayed together, for example, ostriches with giraffes.

The zoo boasts the world's largest colony of orang utans, great apes from Borneo and Sumatra, the result of a very successful breeding program. The name means "man of the jungle" in Malay. The most famous of these creatures is Ah Meng, who takes tea with visitors at 4 p.m. and is also up for breakfast at 9 a.m.

The zoo is extensive and pleasant to walk around but there is a tram if you are hot or tired, and plenty of little kiosks serving drinks and snacks. Look out for the various animal shows and the special exhibit enclosure.

To get back to town either take bus No. 171 to Orchard Road or a taxi.

5. Mixed Heritage

A walk which gives an insight into the Singaporean cultural mix.

Start at about 10 a.m. or an hour earlier if a visit to the **Istana** is possible (on New Year's Day, Chinese New Year, Hari Raya and Deepavali). Take a taxi to Mohamed Sultan Road, just off River Valley Road, and about 200 metres (660 ft) on the right you will see the **Hong San See Temple**, built in 1908. It is reminiscent of Thian Hock Keng Temple in Chinatown, but much more peaceful. There are similar elaborate carvings and stone columns. The main deity is Kok Seng Wang, the Lord of Benefice.

Then cross River Valley Road, turn right, and browse in the antique shops as you make your way to Tank Road. On your left is the **Sri Thandayuthapani Temple**, usually known as the **Chettiar Temple**, as it was built by the Chettiar community in the 1850s, and rebuilt in 1984. The temple, dedicated to Murugan, is especially crowded during the annual Thaipusam Festival (in February) and Navrathri (in September). It boasts 48 glass panel friezes, each etched with a Hindu deity.

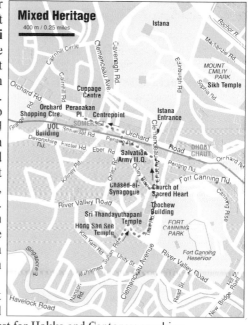

Leave the temple and turn left up Tank Road. You'll come to the **Teochew Building**, a mixture of Chinese and western influence.

Next door make a brief halt at the **Church of the Sacred Heart** designed by a French priest for Hakka and Cantonese speaking members of the Roman Catholic congregation.

Continue up the road until you come to Oxley Rise, where you will see off-white, classical **Chesed-El Synagogue**.

Retrace your steps to the intersection and take Clemenceau Avenue. At the corner of Penang Road is the **Salvation Army Headquarters.** The building is interesting, not for its present function, but for its intricate architecture and history behind it. It was the town house of the wealthy Chinese merchant Tan Yeok Nee, built with granite columns and carvings from China in traditional Southern Chinese style.

51

The Chettiar Temple

After a variety of owners, the Salvation Army acquired it in 1940. From 1942 to 1945, the Japanese Army took it over, the more peaceful army retaking possession after the war.

From here you'll see the white gates and uniformed guard of the **Istana** ("Palace" in Malay) which is the official residence of the President of Singapore. If it is open it is well worth a visit.

Otherwise continue to your left, along Penang Road, turning right onto Orchard Road, where you walk along to your left until you reach the pastel buildings of **Peranakan Place** on your right.

Walk through the terrace cafe to the **Peranakan Place Museum** on the right. It closes at noon so leave yourself half an hour at least for a fascinating tour of a typical Peranakan house of the turn of the century. You'll learn the history of these Peranakans, also known as Straits Chinese, who settled in Malaya and intermarried with the Malays, creating their own unique culture.

Their language was a mixture of Malay and Chinese known as Baba Malay. The men are known as *Baba*s and the women as *Nonya*s, and although nowadays they are no longer a separate group you can appreciate their culture through their decorative houses, and their handiwork in intricate embroidery, lovely porcelain, silverware and furniture.

A peek into our Peranakan past

As you might expect in Singapore it is the Nonya cuisine which is the most popular vestige of these people. A wonderful mixture of influences of Malay, Chinese and Indian ways of cooking make this food eagerly sought after today.

Emerald Hill is a fascinating street, with an interesting antique

52

Sentry at the main gate to the Istana

shop and wonderful old houses to look at. **Apa Villa**, a beautifully restored Peranakan house, holds interesting art exhibitions of local and foreign works. Go in for a look.

There are plenty of places to have lunch here and in Centrepoint and Cuppage Road beyond, so wander around and take your pick from Japanese, Nonya, Italian, Indian or Thai, to name but a few.

You're in the right area for an afternoon's shopping with an enormous selection of shops including Robinson's and Marks and Spencer in Centrepoint. Cuppage Road is well worth exploring too, not missing the upper level of shops and galleries. There's a wet market right at the end of Cuppage Road selling fresh fruit and flowers, as well as meat, fish and vegetables. You can try local food at the food stalls above. It's an interesting part of town, and you may well enjoy spending the whole afternoon here.

6. A Walk in the Jungle

Back in time, back to nature, to primary rainforest millions of years old.

There's not much left in the way of jungle in Singapore, but it is still possible to spend a few hours walking through primary forest. The **Bukit Timah Nature Reserve** encompasses the highest hill on the island, but as it is only 162½ metres (534 ft) above sea level, you won't need mountaineering skills to reach the summit.

This jungle is real, but rather too civilised, with dustbins, benches, man-made steps and even a tarred main road. It's a good idea to bring a bottle of water, a hand towel, mosquito repellent and antihistamine cream. Wear sensible shoes, of course.

It is possible that you'll come across a scorpion, python or black cobra, but it's not very likely. However, don't try Tarzan tricks on the lianas, just in case!

Take a taxi to the reserve, which is off Upper Bukit Timah Road at Hindhede Drive, which should cost about S$8, or take a bus. Buses which serve the area are 5, 75, 170, 171, 172, 173, 179, 180, 181, 182 and 852.

At the entrance is the Ranger's Office, where you can buy a very useful guide for just 60 cents. If there is no-one there, or no stock of the booklets, don't worry as a large map of the area is posted at the entrance, as well as at regular

The route to exploring nature

intervals during your walk.

The four indicated routes are marked in different colours, the yellow route being the longest, taking about 2½ hours to complete. The light blue walk takes about 1½ hours, the red less than an hour and the purple about 40 minutes. You can of course combine different coloured routes, and explore the place as you like. From the summit you'll have a glorious view of Seletar Reservoir.

Traffic and the 20th century recede as you set off up the path into the forest. Little sunlight filters through the canopy of tropical dipterocarps and legumes. Epiphytes and orchids perch high above as spikey rattan and spiralling lianas clamber upwards. Below, shiny palms and gentle ferns grow amid spreading roots and buttresses. On the forest floor, fungi, algae and mosses form a soft carpet. You are surrounded by the deafening insects' chorus punctuated by piercing bird calls.

High above you might spot a Brahminy Kite or a Fish Eagle. Keep your eyes open for the golden flash of a Black-naped Oriole, the iridescent blue of the White-throated Kingfisher or the swooping tail streamers of the Greater Racket-tailed Drongo. Lepidopterists will recognise plenty of Common Grass Yellow and Birdwing butterflies but there are many more interesting species fluttering through the foliage. Keep your eyes peeled for the Idea or Common Tree Nymph and the lovely Great Mormon.

Watch carefully when the leaves rustle. It might be squirrels or

even Long-tailed Macaques. Look out for shiny, emerald green spiders hanging in dew-spangled webs. Scan the forest floor for beetles and ants carrying their booty home.

If you see a lizard fly, it won't be the effects of a late

night, but really a flying dragon (Draco), whose foldable gliding membrane enables it to glide up to 30 metres (99 ft).

See if you can find the insect-eating Pitcher Plant nestling among the leaves. Flowers are few and far between, but you might spot some coloured petals amid the green foliage.

Stop, look and listen to nature. You are in a patch of the type of forest which once covered the whole island, and most of South East Asia. This is what saving the rainforests and conservation is all about!

7. The National Museum

Vivid tableaux and fascinating exhibits bringing history alive.

On Stamford Road stands a splendid classical building surmounted by a gleaming dome. This is the National Museum, which has recently been renovated. It was designed by Major J. F. McNair, and originally opened in Queen Victoria's Jubilee Year.

Now home to a fascinating collection of artefacts from all over Asia, it is well worth a visit. Singapore's early days are recreated in bright dioramas; recorded commentaries explain the cultural heritage of the island and numerous collections and exhibits recreate the Colonial, immigrant and Japanese periods in Singapore's history. Restored costumes, furniture and utensils show Chinese, Malay, Indian and Peranakan households at the turn of the century.

River ride in Haw Par Villa

The **Art Gallery** next door holds works of local artists, and in the shop at the exit you will find excellent reproductions of early water colours of Singapore on blank cards at 50 cents each.

The museum is open from 9 a.m. to 4.30 p.m., the Art Gallery from 9 a.m. to 5.30 p.m.. Both are closed on Mondays.

8. Haw Par Villa

Gaudy, grotesque and gory recreations of hell, earth and heaven.
For a truly exotic, "out of this world" experience, visit the new **Haw Par Villa**. Here Chinese myths, legends and history are brought to life in extraordinary, vividly-coloured figures and scenes, as well as by state-of- the-art shows and exhibitions.

Admission is S$16 for adults, S$10 for children, which includes all kinds of spectacular shows and rides, such as the "Wrath of the Water Gods Flume Ride" which certainly cools you down on a hot day ... and a boat ride into the mouth of a dragon and on through hell!

The garden is open from 9 a.m. to 6 p.m. every day, and is at 262 Pasir Panjang Road over on the west coast of the island.

As the park has only recently opened, it does get extremely crowded at weekends.

P.M. Itineraries

1. Historical Hike

From Museums to Memorials, up Forbidden Hill and down the Singapore River on the trail of Singapore's past.

History buffs might like to make this an all day affair by starting off with a morning at the National Museum for an insight into the story of Singapore which will be explored later.

Art lovers who have noticed beautiful cards of local scenes painted by English artist Graham Byfield should start this tour early by visiting his gallery. At the corner of Hill Street and Stamford Road, next to the MPH "The Courtyard" bookshop, is **Eu Court**, a beautifully restored 1920s building. **The Graham Byfield Gallery,** housing a collection of his original works as well as a selection of cards and small prints, is up on the first floor, but do telephone 339-6630 before you go.

Now for lunch right off the beaten track. Ujagar Singh's cosy restaurant is in Saint Gregory's Place, a side alley off Hill Street, just opposite the U.S. Embassy. At shophouse No. 7, a small sign says "Indian Food Upstairs". You'll soon see why this place is so popular with locals. With mutton chops at S$2, chicken curry at S$3.50 and kebabs at S$1 you can feast like a rajah for under S$10.

After lunch cross the road to the **Armenian Church, Saint Gregory the Illuminator**, the oldest church in Singapore. It is a masterpiece of design by George Dromgold Coleman, and may well have been inspired by St. Martin-in-the-Fields in London, as well as its mother church in Erevan.

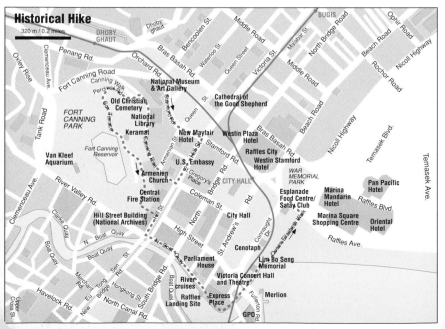

Historical Hike

The Armenian Church

G. D. Coleman, an Irish architect, first came to Singapore in 1822, having worked in India and Batavia (present day Djakarta). It was then that he designed and built the *attap*-roofed Residency on Fort Canning Hill for Sir Stamford Raffles. Coleman returned to Java in 1823, where he remained for two years, returning to Singapore at the outbreak of war between the Dutch colonists and the Javanese people. He went on to design and build major government buildings, mansions and godowns in Neo-Classical style (described more fully in the Day 1 itinerary). His 1822 design for the first Church of St. Andrew was eventually implemented in 1835, and the church completed 2 years later.

Walk around the churchyard and pause at the gravestone of Agnes Joaquim, who found and gave her name to the national flower, a large purple hybrid orchid. Here too lie the Sarkies brothers who established Raffles Hotel in 1887.

At the exit turn right into Canning Rise and make your way to the white gateway of **Fort Canning Park.** By the time Raffles arrived in Singapore in 1819, this hill this was known as Bukit Larangan (Forbidden Hill) as it was rumoured to be haunted by spirits of the Majapahit princes from Java who ruled from here in the 14th century.

The last of these five rulers, Iskandar Shah, Prince of Palembang in Sumatra, is said to be buried here, although there is some doubt as to whether his remains are indeed in the tomb which may be seen today.

Due to its strategic view over the Straits, this part of the island was a centre of activity in the early years and you might have seen finds from here in the museum.

Raffles, undeterred by supersti-

Reconstruction of Raffles Hotel will be completed by 1991

tion or spirits, erected Coleman's wood and *attap* house up on the hill which was later renamed Government Hill. He also founded the first botanical gardens here, planting cocoa and spices, but this was closed in 1829.

In 1857 the military took over, building Fort Canning which was completed in 1860. This was a disaster as the enemy ships at sea were out of range of the guns, which if fired would only have destroyed the town. They did serve, however to announce at noon to the populace as well as dawn and dusk. The fort was demolished in 1907, and the hilltop is now a reservoir.

Through the gateway you will reach the first Christian cemetery in Singapore, great big gravestones huddled in a corner. Follow the path through a similar gateway to the ASEAN (Association of South-East Asian Nations) sculpture garden established in 1981. Keep straight on unless you branch off to see the tomb. Look out for a small bunker where General Percival, commander of the British forces is said to have decided on the surrender of Singapore, after the Japanese had cut off the island's water supply in February 1942.

You then go past remnants of the wall and through the old fort entrance. Follow the path ahead to the lookout point, walking beneath wonderful old trees as you listen to the hum of insects competing with city traffic.

A flight of stairs will lead you down to the former Hill Street Police Station, which now houses the **National Archives.** If you go in the first door you come to on the right and up to the first floor, you'll find the library where postcards of the past may be purchased at S$2.50 per set. The Singapore River pictures will enable you to compare past and present as you cross River Valley Road and walk downriver under the Coleman and Elgin Bridges.

The river is now clean and devoid of the old bumboats, which used to ply between the ships in the harbour and the godowns on the river bank. New

Cruising down Singapore River

Reflections of old shop-houses in the river

shopping centres vie for space with tumbledown shophouses, some now being renovated as the area gains popularity with companies looking for interesting office space.

At the little kiosk just past Elgin Bridge, buy a S$6 ticket for a half hour **River Cruise**. The boats leave roughly on the hour. Take a leisurely ride upriver and then out into the harbour, with a recorded commentary. Just sit back and take a trip to the past.

Back on land make your way back along North Boat Quay, past Raffles' statue at the point he first landed in 1819 to the riverside terrace of the imposing green and white **Empress Place Building** and have a refreshing drink there or at the food stalls further along.

Then go inside the beautifully restored building, for years housed dingy government offices, now a museum which features a permanent exhibition from China. Entrance costs S$6 and the museum stays open until 9.30 p.m. Interesting shops sell Chinese ceramics, silks and a range of teas as well as all kinds of other souvenirs.

In **Empress Place** is the **Dalhousie Memorial**, built to commemorate a visit to Singapore by the Governor General of India, the

Fountain figurines

Marquis of Dalhousie. Beyond is **Cavenagh Bridge** with the **Victoria Memorial Hall and Theatre** on the left.

Take the underpass to **Queen Elizabeth Walk** in **Esplanade Park** with the symbol of Singapore, the **Merlion,** on your right. On your left across the **Padang** are the colonial buildings of the **Supreme Court, City Hall** and **St. Andrew's Cathedral** all described in the Day 1 itinerary.

You'll pass the **Lim Bo Seng Memorial**. During World War II. He was a resistance leader of Force 136 in Malaya and was brutally tortured to death by the Japanese.

Further on is the **Cenotaph**, a memorial to Singapore men killed in World War I, with the names of the World War II dead being added later. This was unveiled in 1922 by the Prince of Wales, later the Duke of Windsor. He was accompanied by Lord Louis Mountbatten, who returned in 1945 as Supreme Allied Commander South East Asia, to take the surrender of the Japanese.

Across Stamford Road you'll see four tapering pillars of the **War Memorial**, locally known as the "Chopsticks", which symbolise the civilians of the four main racial groups who died at the hands of the Japanese during the occupation during World War II.

By now you'll have gained a deeper understanding of how Singapore became what it is today.

To round off the evening you could return to Empress Place for a Chinese dinner or sit outside at the Satay Club. But while you are at this end of town, why not explore **Marina Village** (see our *Nightlife* chapter).

Singapore River at sunset

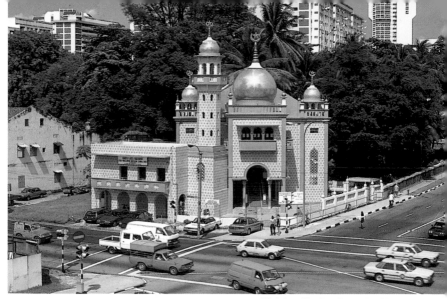

Malabar Muslim Jama-Ath Mosque

2. Kampong Glam

A walk around the Malay part of town, looking at mosques and a treasure trove of batik, baskets, bangles and beads.

Take a taxi to the corner of Beach Road and **Arab Street**, not forgetting to be properly dressed if you wish to enter the mosques.

This area of **Kampong Glam** was designated by Sir Stamford Raffles for Arabs and Muslims. The name is derived from "Kampong" which means village in Malay, and the "Glam" tree, the *Melaleuca Leucadendron*, with spirally arranged, narrow leaves and white flowers. The bark was prized for its medicinal values, as well as being used by the Bugis and Malays to caulk their ships. The shophouses are as designated by Raffles, with the five-foot way for shelter now a handy extension to the shops and a boon to people walking in the heat.

You'll find the best selection of rattan and basketware right on the corner. Further along are kaftans and sarongs and wonderful leather goods, as well as lace, tablecloths and prayer mats. Whatever you buy here will be cheaper than in the centre of town, and you can bargain.

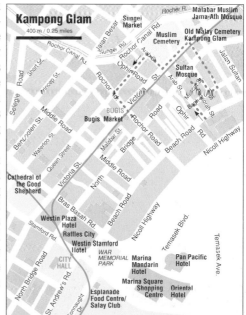

Sultan Mosque

Turn right into **Baghdad Street**, then left into **Bussorah Street** and you will have a magnificent view of the **Sultan Mosque**, which was completed in 1928 and is one of over 80 mosques in Singapore. You might hear the muezzin calling the faithful at prayer time.

Go inside and enjoy the feel of the soft, attractive carpet donated by Saudi Arabia. Upstairs is where the women remain during worship.

At the exit, turn left and make your way to the old yellowish house ahead, going along **Kandahar Street**, with its lovely old pastel buildings, left onto **Baghdad Street** and then left again at the junction of Baghdad Street and **Sultan Gate**.

You will then come to the **Istana Kampong Glam.** Now falling into disrepair, it was once the palace of Sultan Ali Iskandar Shah, son of the first sultan of Singapore, Sultan Hussein. It was he who together with Temenggong Daeng Ibrahim ceded Singapore to the East India Company for the sum of 5,000 Spanish dollars a year, plus this compound.

You can't go in, unfortunately, as the place is still lived in by descendants of the Sultan, who are numerous it seems, so just take the alleyway on the right of the Istana out onto **North Bridge Road.**

Cross over and take Jalan Kubor through to **Victoria Street.** There on the right is the blue, traditional style **Malabar Muslim Jama-Ath Mosque**. The prayer room is upstairs, and from the gallery you can look down on the quiet palm shaded cemetery behind.

Turn right as you come out, go back down Victoria Street and you will pass the oldest Muslim cemetery in Singapore, where the graves are arranged under the sweet smelling frangipani trees. Records as far back as 1836 show that Malay Princes were buried here.

Cross over Arab Street and Ophir Road and you'll come to a shop of bright red and gold religious artefacts, with all kinds of statues, brass and jade for sale. Next along is the maker of intricate altars and then you can see teak barrels made in the old style. It's a place where you can sometimes see craftsmen at work and might find unusual souvenirs.

Just along on the other side of the road is the MRT station.

Majestic Siong Lim Shan Sze Temple

3. Toa Payoh New Town, Temple and a Revolutionary's Villa

Get right off the beaten track: meet Singaporeans in a New Town; visit a Chinese temple in that neighbourhood; gain an insight into Sun Yat Sen's activities in his headquarters.

Either take a taxi directly to **Lian Shan Siong Lim Shan Sze**, or The Twin Grove of the Lotus Mountain Buddhist Temple, or ride the cool, pristine MRT on the North Line to **Toa Payoh**. At the exit is the bus station, where numbers 26, 142 and 149 go to, the largest Buddhist temple in Singapore. The name commemorates Buddha's birth in a wooded grove, and his death between two Bodhi trees.

Wander around the spacious interior and observe worshippers repeatedly bowing in prayer with incense sticks between their palms, or sitting silent meditation beneath the beautiful ceiling. The marble Buddhas from Thailand are impressive, as is the large golden laughing Buddha. The garden with its great rocks is peaceful, but less extensive than when the temple was built, as half the land area was donated to the Housing and Development Board years ago for low-cost housing.

The resulting flats are the type in which the majority of Singa-

poreans live today, as the government clears away most of the less hygienic, if more romantic *kampongs* or villages. Long external corridors lead to individual flats, which often reflect the race of the occupants; the Chinese display red banners, or lanterns outside, and Indians have pictures of their deities above the door.

Cross the road and take the bus back to the interchange. Just across Lorong 6 Toa Payoh you'll see a small red and white tower in a park. **Toa Payoh Town Garden** is a peaceful oasis of ponds and willows, shady angsanas, bamboo and flowering trees. Created by the Housing Board in the early years of development even though land was scarce, it a pleasant place to relax. Climb up the tower and have a look around.

At the other end of the park by Toa Payoh Seafood Restaurant, where you might like a freshly squeezed fruit juice, is a footbridge. As you cross it, you'll see a pale yellow colonial bungalow to the right, the **Sun Yat Sen Villa.** A typical colonial bungalow of the early 20th century, it blends Palladian with Chinese and Malay architecture, with wide verandahs, high ceilings and servants' quarters at the back. The caretaker speaks no English but will let you in free. Pick up a booklet.

Originally named Bin Chan House, it became the headquarters of Dr. Sun Yat Sen and his communist revolutionaries in the 1910s on his visits to Singapore. It was here that he finalised many plans for the overthrow of the Manchu dynasty in China.

His life and exploits are traced in old photographs, letters and maps downstairs. Upstairs is a moving display of photos and possessions of those who endured, life in Syonan-to, as Singapore was known during the 3½ years of Japanese occupation. From here retrace your steps to the Town Garden and perhaps have supper by

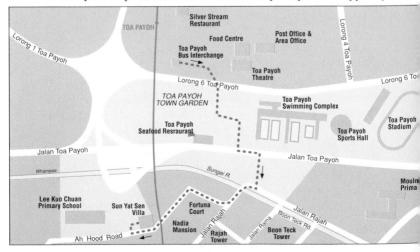

The Botanic Gardens, the perfect place to relax in on a hot afternoon

the lake. There are plenty of cheap restaurants and shops to explore, so there's no need to leave the local scene too early.

4. The Botanic Gardens

A pleasant stroll through soothing green; lush greenery, a vivid orchid garden and peaceful parkland

Where Holland Road and Napier Road join, just 10 minutes walk from Orchard Road, a white gateway leads into beautiful gardens, more than five times as old as the nation itself. The Botanic Gardens, which extend over 32 hectares (80 acres), contain over 3,000 species of trees and shrubs, in areas as varied as virgin jungle, marshland, lakes and formal gardens. It is here that the first rubber trees in Asia were grown, from which Henry Ridley started the rubber industry of Malaysia. Most trees are named, so you learn as you go along.

In the orchid you can see exactly how orchids are grown from seed. There are more than 2,500 plants with 250 different hybrids here, including Singapore's national flower, the purple Vanda Miss Joachim. A riot of glorious colour, this spectacular garden is often crowded with wedding parties taking photographs.

By the time it gets light, at around 7 a.m., the gardens will already have been open for 2 hours, and it's a place best seen

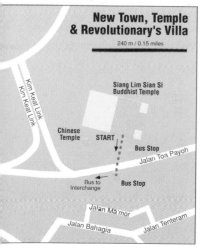

New Town, Temple & Revolutionary's Villa

240 m / 0.15 miles

Kim Keat Link
Kim Keat Link

Siang Lim Sian Si Buddhist Temple

Chinese Temple START

Bus Stop

Jalan Toa Payoh

Bus to Interchange   Bus Stop

Jalan Ma mor

Jalan Bahagia   Jalan Tenteram

67

early before the coaches arrive. Dawn is also when you will see health-conscious Singaporeans doing *Tai C'hi,* a graceful Chinese martial art.

5. Sentosa

An afternoon on the most organised of Singapore's offshore islands.

You are invited to discover the different "worlds" of **Sentosa**, and whether your penchant is for history, nature or simply fun for the kids, the island offers a contrast to the hustle and bustle city atmosphere of Singapore.

Take a taxi to the World Trade Centre. Buy a one-way ticket to Sentosa on the cable car, and enjoy the splendid view of the port and Keppel Shipyard. Sentosa was once known as "Blakang Mati" which means "Back of the Dead", as it was where the local pirates buried their victims. Nowadays it is a leisure spot for tourists and locals alike.

Once on the island you can decide which kind of entry ticket you prefer. The S$8 ticket includes entry to most attractions.

Turn left from the ticket booth and visit the **Pioneers of Singapore** exhibition, which will give you a fascinating insight into the development of Singapore from its earliest days and coolie life, to Mad Ridley and his rubber, Miss Joaquim and her orchid right up to the present day.

The ferry terminal on Sentosa Island

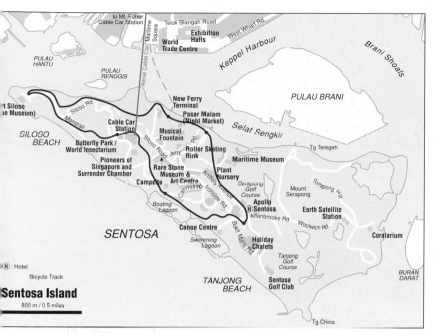

The adjoining **Surrender Chamber** takes you through the years of World War II with waxworks depicting surrender first by the British in 1942, then by the Japanese in 1945.

If you are interested in butterflies, the pretty park opposite costs just S$2.50 to enter. Otherwise take the monorail to **Fort Siloso** and continue in historical vein.

Then back on the monorail to station 1. Alight and look at the beautiful formal gardens.

You can then continue your exploration of the island by bus or monorail, all well sign-posted. But by far the most pleasant way to enjoy the place is by hiring a bicycle (S$3 per hour), and just peddling from one place to another along shady jungle paths.

When you return your bike, have a drink or some local food at the stalls of the **Rasa Sentosa** and wander around the stalls of the night market as it slowly comes to life in the evening.

The fascinating musical fountain display starts at 7.30 p.m. Or, if you take the ferry back to the World Trade Centre at around 5.30 p.m. you'll be just in time to take a sunset cruise.

Madame Tussaud figures of Singapore's surrender to the Japanese

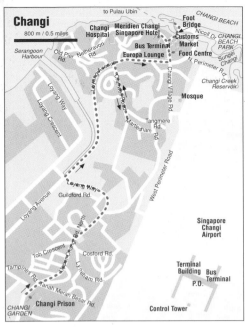

to Pulau Ubin

Changi
800 m / 0.5 miles

CHANGI BEACH

Foot Bridge
Changi Hospital
Meridien Changi Singapore Hotel
Nicoll Dr.
CHANGI BEACH PARK
Customs
Bus Terminal
Market
Serangoon Harbour
Old Pier Rd.
Netheravon Rd.
Europa Lounge
Food Centre
Sungei Changi
N. Perimeter Rd.
Loyang Way
Changi Village Rd.
Changi Creek Reservoir
Loyang Crescent
Netheravon Rd.
Mosque
Marileaham
Tangmere Rd.
West Perimeter Road
Loyang Way
Loyang Avenue
Guildford Rd.
Singapore Changi Airport
Toh Crescent
Upper Changi Rd. North
Cosford Rd.
Lyneham Rd.
Terminal Building
P.O.
Bus Terminal
Tampines Rd.
Tanah Merah Besar Rd.
CHANGI GARDEN
Changi Prison
Control Tower

6. Changi

A visit to the east of the island in remembrance of prisoners of World War II. We go to the Changi Prison Chapel and Museum and then look at the famous Changi Murals. Afterwards a stroll along the beach and perhaps a boat ride over to Pulau Ubin.

Take a taxi to **Changi Prison**, which will cost about S$15. If you just want to visit the museum and chapel and then return, ask the driver to wait for you.

The museum is just to the left of the main gate of the forbidding looking edifice of the prison. It is open from 2 until 4.30 on weekday afternoons, from 8.30 to 12.30 on weekday mornings and on Saturdays, and from 3.30 to 5.30 on Sundays. A service is held

in the Chapel from 5.30 to 6.30 on Sunday evenings. There is a little shop selling a good selection of books on the war period as well as souvenirs.

The museum gives a moving insight into life as a Prisoner of War in Changi Prison, which eventually housed 3,000 prisoners. W.R.M. Haxworth's drawings and George Aspinall's photographs once seen will never be forgotten. Nor will the suffering of the POWs. In the little **Prison Chapel**, cards expressing fond memories and gratitude are affixed to a board to the left of the altar, and you are invited to pick a flower from the garden and place it on the altar in remembrance of these brave men who fought during the war.

To visit the **Changi Murals** in Selarang Barracks, turn right out of the gate and drive straight on, over the crossroads and follow the road as it bends left as Loyang Way, until you reach Loyang Avenue, where you make a right turn. Eventually you will find Cranwell Road on the right, which leads to Martlesham Road where at the Guardroom of block 122 you may ask for the key to the Murals. You may be escorted to Block 151, where despite difficulties in acquiring materials, Stanley Warren painted five beautiful murals

depicting scenes from the life of Christ.

After the war, the murals, covered with distemper, were almost forgotten, but interest was later aroused and Mr. Warren was finally located in London and persuaded to come to Singapore to restore them in 1963, and to do further work in 1982. Now the former chapel is again a place of worship, and a tribute to men's faith under duress.

Turn right out of Cranwell Road and then take Changi Village Road to the left. On the corner is George Photo, where George Aspinall learned how to develop photographs. Round to the left you will come to the Changi Meridien Hotel. Here you might like a drink, and on the 5th Floor is an exhibition with more reproductions of George Aspinall's photographs and details of the Murals and information about World War II.

Changi Beach

To explore this end of the island, retrace your steps to George Photo where you turn left to the bus terminal and car park. Cross the little bridge and take the footpath to **Changi Beach**, deserted mainly during the week, packed at weekends. It's a lovely place to wander at leisure away from the bustle of the city, watching the ships sailing to and from the port.

If you feel like a boat trip, make your way back over the bridge and down to the jetty at **Changi Point** on your right. There are always plenty of boatmen ready to go to **Pulau Ubin**, the island you saw over to the left from the beach. Usually you wait for twelve passengers and pay S$1 each to get there, but you can make up the difference and bargain. Getting back costs the same again.

Over on Pulau Ubin take a taxi to see around the island, which is still rustic, although soon to be developed. Walk around the village, and if you like, stay for supper in the seafood restaurant.

Back in Singapore, you might like to enjoy "Happy Hour" at the Europa Lounge at the corner of Changi Village Road, and then perhaps a taste of local dishes in the food centre in Changi Village before taking a taxi or bus No. 14 back to Orchard Road. Otherwise drive along the East Coast Parkway on your way back to the centre, and eat at any of the innumerable restaurants serving fresh, delicious seafood.

Lanterns light the way in the Chinese Gardens

7. The Chinese and Japanese Gardens

Two distinctly different, equally lovely gardens side by side.
Take the MRT to the Chinese Garden Station for a ride which takes you above ground for much of the way out to Jurong in the west of the island.

The cost of entrance to both gardens which are open from 9 a.m. to 7 p.m. daily is S$2.50 for adults, S$1.20 for children and 50 cents for a camera.

The Chinese Garden is modelled on the Imperial Sung Dynasty style like the Peking Summer Palace. Bridges and archways harmonise with nature and its exotic lakeside pagodas offer a glorious view of the gardens. You can walk along the banks of the lake, or even go out in a little boat.

Wander around the Herb Garden, the Ixora Garden where these lovely bright flowering shrubs are featured and the Garden of Fragrance.

Then take the 65-metre (214 ft) long bridge over to the **Japanese Garden,** also called **The Garden of Tranquility**, which is just what it is. Small shrubs, stone lanterns and a miniature waterfall induce a feeling of serenity. There is also a traditional tea house.

These two gardens show different Oriental approaches to horticulture and nature itself and give an insight into two different and distinct cultures.

8. Getting High

Relaxation and refreshment with a sweeping panorama.
For a bird's eye view of Singapore and beyond, in the **Mandarin Hotel** in Orchard Road, there's the **Observation Lounge**, a circular

bar open from 11 a.m. until 1 a.m. and on the floor above, the **Top of the M** restaurant for dinner in the evening.

Higher still is the **Compass Rose** in the **Westin Stamford Hotel**, the tallest hotel tower in the world. On the 70th floor of **Raffles City**, the bar is open from 11 a.m. until 1 a.m. where a seafood buffet lunch is served during the week. You can see right to Malaysia and Indonesia, and sunset from here is spectacular. Dinner in the restaurant gives you a view over the Singapore River and the city lights.

Just across the road in the **Pan Pacific Hotel** is the Hai Tien Lo Cantonese restaurant, reached by an elevator on the outside of the building.

Up in the gleaming triangular tower of the OUB Building in the city is **The Pinnacle**, a restaurant where you look down at the river and over to the west from the 60th floor while choosing from a menu which cleverly combines the cuisines of both east and west.

A favourite local haunt is the Chinese **Prima Tower Revolving Restaurant** up on the Flourmill near the World Trade Centre, where you choose from a selection of little delicacies for an excellent dim sum lunch and a la carte at dinner. The restaurant takes 2 hours to go round, giving you a splendid view of the harbour and Mount Faber.

For reservations call 272-8988.

Nightlife

1. Night Out at Newton

Supper under the stars.

No visit to Singapore would be complete without a visit to the hawker stalls, and the creme de la creme are to be found at **Newton Circus**. So dress in cool, casual clothes, take the MRT to Newton station, and make your way to the open-air food centre.

You'll see bright lights under the fly-over, cars queueing, buses disgorging visitors of all nationalities and locals strolling along discussing exactly which is their favourite food, and which stall gives best value for money.

Take your time, and just wander around first. There are 88 stalls here and the choice of food and drink is mind-boggling. Just see who has what you fancy, be it Chinese, Indian or Malay, or fresh crabs, lobster or giant prawns cooked any way you like.

There are so many kinds of food to whet your appetite, from fresh fish, cockles, mussels, oysters (usually priced by the 100 gm) to delicious satay sticks of marinated beef, chicken or mutton. Then there's Malay *nasi padang* (about S$4 for rice with your choice from a wide range of delicious accompanying dishes). Noodles of all shapes, sizes and flavours, fish porridge and *nasi goreng*, you name it, it's definitely here somewhere.

The place is buzzing with action – Indians whirling *prata*, Chinese tossing *mee*, steaming pots and bubbling woks, and flummoxed women bearing plates of delicious food, desperately looking for the customer.

When you have finally made your choice, sit down and place your order. Large bottles of Anchor Beer cost S$6, but you might like to sip a fresh coconut or even bring your own wine. You pay when the food arrives

(NO TIPPING PLEASE).

Finish the meal with fried bananas or fresh rambutans, durians, mangosteens or whatever fresh fruit is in season.

Sitting outside under the angsana trees at Newton Circus, you'll have a feast, and not be penniless at the end of the evening!

2. Cruises at Sunset and After

Cruising in style and comfort.

Getting offshore is part of the fun of island life, and the choice ranges from packed Chinese junk tours to the airconditioned catamaran, the *Equator Dream.*

There are cruises all day long, but it's hard to beat watching the sun set as you float past Singapore's coast and offshore islands. As the sun sets at about seven in the evening, the best option is the "Sunset Cruise" on the *Equator Dream* which leaves the World Trade Centre at 6 p.m. and costs S$70 inclusive of a buffet dinner. The later "Romantic Dinner Cruise" leaves at 8.30 p.m. and you can stay on board to dance for a while, or for S$20 leave on the late night "Rendezvous Disco Cruise" which returns at midnight, although you can dance on, until 1 a.m. usually, or for S$30 until 2 a.m. on Fridays, Saturdays and Eve of Public Holiday nights. Contact J&N Cruises Tel: 270-7100. The ticket office is at the World Trade Centre.

If you would like to be collected from your hotel, you might prefer the smaller *Raffles Princess.* Transport is included in the charge of S$65 for a 2½-hour cruise leaving the World Trade Centre

Romantic sunset harbour cruise

at 7 p.m. with a buffet supper, and a visit to the **Musical Fountain** on **Sentosa Island.** Call Creative Cruises Tel: 473-3233.

Small bumboats may also be hired from Clifford Pier, where you negotiate your own terms, so do take the opportunity to look at Singapore from the sea.

3. Dinner at the Alkaff Mansion

Go back in time to the good old days of the 1920s and dine in an elegant mansion overlooking the Straits of Singapore.

Take a taxi to the **Alkaff Mansion** up on Mount Faber Ridge in time to enjoy sundowners out on the terrace. There, relaxing in the tropical garden, you can take in the glorious view of the harbour and city of Singapore.

Gracious dining at
Alkaff Mansion

When the sun has set, go inside for dinner. You'll feel as if you are the guest in a spacious private house. The high ceilings with silent fans make the interior pleasantly cool. Soft wall and standard lamps, lovely prints, rugs on the polished floor, and the dining room where each table is different enhance the atmosphere, so reminiscent of the early years of Singapore life. This is the Singapore of Somerset Maugham and Tanamera!

In the hall downstairs is a curry buffet, while upstairs you can choose from an a la carte continental menu. Best of all, however, is the Rijstaffel. This is a traditional Indonesian meal comprising a total of fifteen spicy dishes. A procession of beautiful ladies in *sarong kebayas* will bring the dishes to you, a feast for the eyes as well as the palate. Just sit back and enjoy the live music, the relaxed, romantic atmosphere, and the gentle, attentive service.

After dinner, sip your nightcap in the verandah bar, or outside under the stars.

For reservations call 278-6979.

4. Pubs and Discos

Music to suit your mood.

Singapore isn't Bangkok, or the risque port it used to be, but you can still have a good time here. Many hotels have discos and if you've ever fancied being a rock star, karaoke lounges are the latest fad, so you can take the mike and see if you can emulate Elvis. Here are some suggestions for an evening's revelry at the top end of Orchard Road.

Start off down in the cellar under the Hyatt Regency Hotel in **Brannigan's**, a pub with videos and live entertainment. Then walk up to Orchard Road, turn right and make your way to the **Orchard Parade Hotel**. You'll probably hear the sounds of guitars and singing from the terrace cafe there.

Just behind the hotel, on the corner of Cuscaden Road, you can see a vintage car bursting from the wall above the entrance to the **Hard Rock Cafe** where you'll be assured of a lively welcome, even if you have to wait a while to get in. You can pass the time listening to the music and watching the smokers' coterie (smoking inside is permitted after 11 p.m. when the kitchen closes).

You'll get a table eventually, and then things move fast. The American food is good, quickly served, and comes in generous portions. Just enjoy the most laid back atmosphere in Singapore and the superb sounds. Before you move on, have a look at the amazing collection of rock memorabilia on the walls.

Now it's time to hit the discos. Just across the road, down underneath the Ming Arcade is the **Hot Line Fun Pub** where the bands are good. You're into cover charge time now, but it's not too much here.

Then go back to Orchard Road to Orchard Towers and look into **Club 392** on the ground floor. If that doesn't appeal, there are plenty more places just in the two towers. Up on level 2 is the spacious **Caesar's** where you can dance and listen to live music, and across the bridge in the other tower is **Ginivy's**, a pub for country and western fans.

Back in the first tower on level 4 you'll see a rock video

on a T.V. screen outside a converted cinema, which is now the **Top Ten**. This is a great place to round off the evening. The local and international bands are good, and there's plenty of bar and dancing space, while the tiered seating makes people-watching easy. So dance the night away, they don't close until 3 a.m.

5. Marina Village

Tucked away on the seashore is Marina Village, Singapore's Fisherman's Wharf, which like the San Francisco original, is a place to while away the hours eating, drinking and listening to musicians.

Off the East Coast Parkway, Marina Village can be reached by taxi or free shuttle buses which run every half hour from 6.30 p.m. to midnight. One route starts up at the Boulevard Hotel, stopping at the major hotels down Orchard Road, and the other sets off from Sheraton Towers, making its way down Scotts Road and on via Marina Square. There's an MRT station at Marina Bay too.

The International Village is a gourmet's delight, a cosy cluster of 6 pubs and 12 restaurants offering delicacies from all over the world. Wander around the village and visit whichever country takes your fancy.

Glittering silver, sumptuous decor and the chance to try *couscous* might entice you to **Marrakech.** Perhaps the **Bouzouki Bar's** gentle tones will beckon you to **Greece, My Love**. Who can resist the little tin Soldier outside **H.C. Andersen,** or the Smorrebrod inside? **Tic Toc** Swiss service or booze in the **Bierstube**? What about **Que? Manuel** for finer fare than Fawlty Towers ever offered? Then Italian, pizza upstairs, or if not, downstairs at **Via Veneto**? Local delights at the stalls of **Makanan Kampung** or Cantonese cuisine in the elegant **Kun Ming**? For the culinary acme, why not wend your way up the winding stairs of the **Ocean Spray** vessel for a voyage to the haute steak and seafood cuisine of Europe?

Then boogie to the band in **Rhythm & Blues** or check out who's on at **Khameleon** to wind up your international evening.

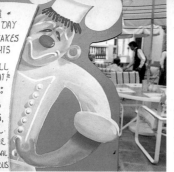

6. Chilli Crabs at Punggol

Less a meal; more an experience. Whole crabs drenched in hot chilli gravy to be bashed with a hammer and prised open with your fingers.

Dress very casually (the gravy gets everywhere so don't wear white). Take a taxi or bus No. 82 or 83 to the end of the road, to the northern tip of **Punggol**. There you'll find a cluster of roadside restaurants looking out at the Straits of Johor, where some of the best chilli and pepper crabs on the island are served. Untamed foliage, sand and dirt open space for free-for-all parking, wobbly wooden tables, plastic plates and chairs, Christmas lights, raucous families and hopeful dogs and cats all create a larger than life throwback to a 1950s family outing.

Pick a restaurant (Choon Seng's my favourite) and order. One medium crab is sufficient for two people, and will cost about S$20, more if you ask for a specially selected premium crab. Pepper crabs are slightly bigger so cost a little more than chilli crabs; a great debate goes on as to which is more delicious. While you're waiting, do try the crispy prawn pancake sprinkled with sesame seeds at S$8 for a medium sized plate.

Local Tiger or Anchor Beer is the best drink with this succulent meal, but you can bring your own wine if you like. No corkage is charged, although you may be asked for a couple of dollars for ice.

Then crack the crustaceans, extract the succulent centre, scoop up the spicy gravy and savour the quintessential taste of Singapore.

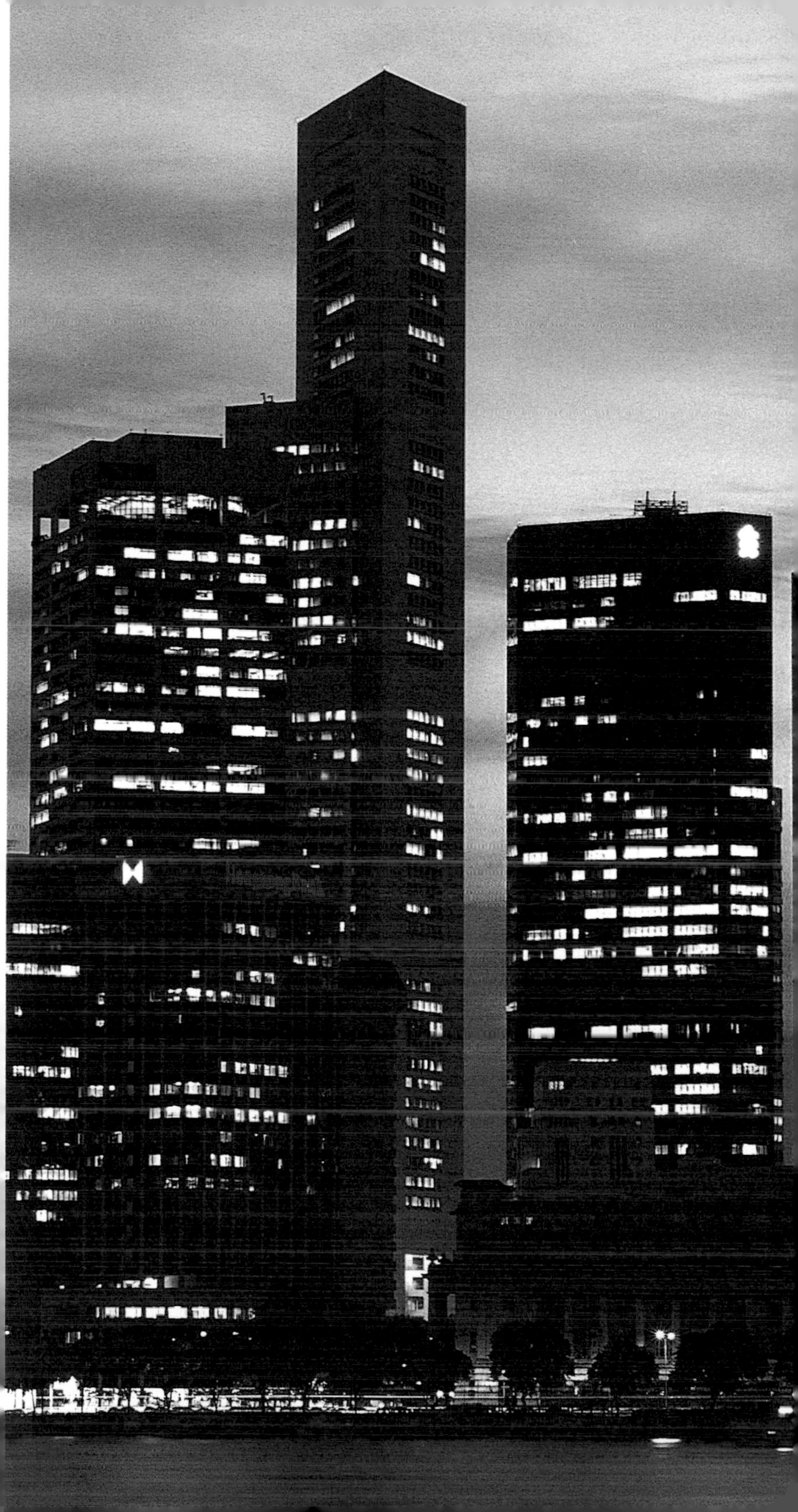

Day TRIPS

1. Johor Baru

A glimpse of Malaysia.

This is a trip away from the bustle of Singapore, an exploration of **Johor Baru**, the southernmost town in Peninsular Malaysia. It is the capital of the **State of Johor**, one of 13 states which, along with Sabah and Sarawak in Borneo, comprise the Federation of Malaysia.

You can hire a car from Singapore, (Avis, Tel: 737-1668). Remember to check that your petrol tank is at least three quarters full before you leave Singapore, as you could be fined S$500 if it isn't. This rule was introduced to prevent loss of revenue in Singapore because petrol is cheaper in Mal aysia.

As most Singapore taxis do not have the necessary permit to take you to Johor, you can call 296-7054/292-0198 for the Singapore-Johor Taxi Service to arrange collection from your hotel and the drive to Johor Baru. Once over there, you will be able to arrange for a taxi for four or five hours at about M$20 per hour. At the end of the day, you can get a cab back over to Singapore again.

Another alternative is to take the Singapore-Johor Express bus

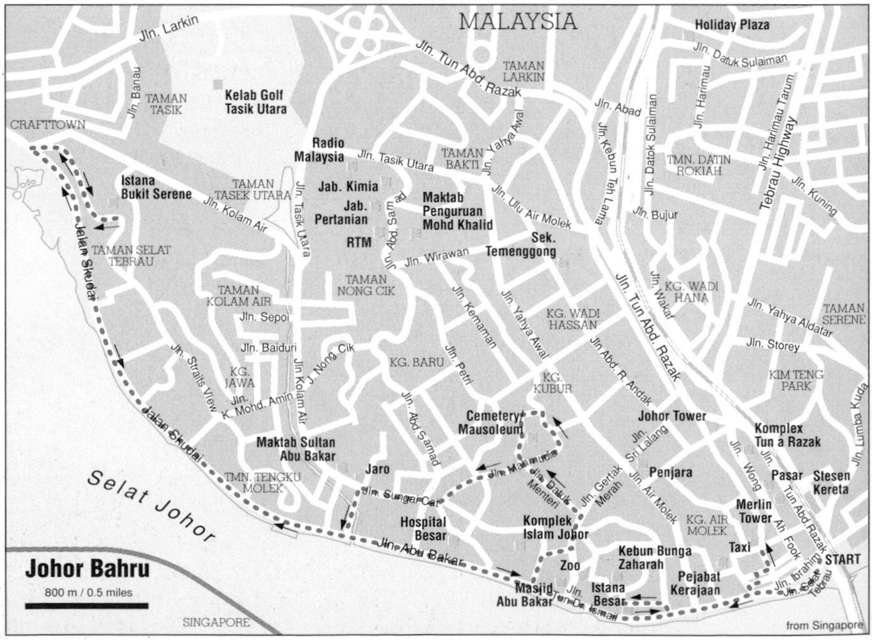

Johor Bahru
800 m / 0.5 miles

The causeway to Johor Baru

which leaves Ban San Street, behind Rochor Centre and Our Lady of Lourdes Church, every seven minutes. The trip costs just S$1.80 to Johor Bus Station, where you can arrange your taxi.

SBS bus No. 170 also goes to Johor Baru from Queen Street Terminal, but stops often on the way.

Don't forget your passport.

If you drive, take the Pan Island Expressway (PIE) then the Bukit Timah Expressway (BKE) to Woodlands. If you prefer, you can drive up Bukit Timah Road, and just past the Jurong Road, on your left, is the Ford Factory, where the British surrender to the Japanese was signed in 1942. Further up towards Woodlands on the right is **Kranji War Cemetery and Singapore State Cemetery**, a moving tribute to those who gave their lives in World War II in South East Asia.

Then you drive across the 1.3-km (8-miles) causeway spanning the motionless waters of the Straits of Johor to Malaysia. This road and rail link was completed in 1924 at a cost of 12 million Straits Dollars, and as you'll see from the lines of lorries, it is vital for trade between Malaysia and Singapore. It's more than that though; it is a major lifeline for Singapore because the enormous pipes you see on your right carry water from Johor to thirsty Singaporeans.

On the other side you will have to fill in an immigration form and pay one M$1 or S$1 for which no change will be given. The Malaysian Ringgit (M$) is lower than the Singapore Dollar (S$), currently at about M$1.50 to S$1. Although most places will accept Singapore Dollars, change will be given in Ringgit and the exchange rates will not be as good as at a money changer. There are plenty of these just along the road into town.

Malaysia is a parliamentary democracy, but there are still nine sultans, who although bereft of political power, remain extremely influential as landowners and heads of religion in their states. They take it in turns to be King of Malaysia for a five year period. The present Sultan

School children at Kranji War Memorial and Cemetery

The court house

Iskandar of Johor was King from 1984 to 1989, and the history of his family is part of the fascination of the place. He is one of the richest men in the world, and has his own army of three hundred soldiers.

You might just hear a siren heralding the outriders on motorbikes who precede the Sultan's motorcade. Keep to the side of the road as he sweeps along the centre which is cleared for him.

Just past the white columns of the court house, you will see an elegant white building with a blue roof, the **Istana Besar** or Grand Palace. At the traffic lights turn right up Jalan Ayer Molek into the spacious grounds of what was until 1936 the residence of the Sultans of Johor. Overlooking the Straits, this lovely palace is now a fascinating museum. It opens at 10 a.m. every day except Friday, when it is closed. The entrance fee to the museum is US$7 for foreigners and M$5 for Malaysians and Singaporeans. You'll have to show your passport when buying your ticket and the exchange rate will be calculated for you. There are guides who will show you round, explain everything and answer all your questions. They don't charge a fee, but if you got the change from your entry ticket in Ringgit, a token would be much appreciated.

You start in the Dewan or hall, where the history of the state is traced from the earliest days of the Johor-Riau-Lingga-Pahang Empire to the present day.

Then you move over to the palace proper and taking your shoes with you in a bag, you can enjoy the feel of the luxurious royal carpets and wonder at the throne room and the family bedrooms. The furnishings are stupendous, and include a Baccarat crystal dining

table and chairs, and elaborately-carved Indian furniture, enormous four poster beds, and sparkling chandeliers. Finally you enter the splendid banqueting hall, ready for a sumptuous feast. It is decked out in the Johor royal colour, yellow, and the British royal colour, blue. Ties with Britain are evident in the many gifts and honours bestowed in the past, as well as in the family tree. In 1935 a Scottish girl became Sultana.

The friendship between the Sultan and Emperor Hirohito, which preserved Johor from destruction during World War II, is also evident in fascinating gifts from Japan, and the replica of a Japanese tea house in the garden.

There are galleries displaying magnificent collections of silver and gold, traditional Malay costumes, and betel nut sets intricately fashioned in silver, and a room with many different kinds of *keris* (the traditional Malay dagger with an undulating blade). In the Hunting Gallery are trophies won at horse racing and hunting. The latter include stag heads, numerous ivory tusks and a huge tiger. This collection is not growing!

Take your time to enjoy the fascinating insight into Johor's past and present. When you leave, you can explore the Japanese garden by the traditional teahouse (not open for tea these days, unfortunately). Otherwise take the path down to the right of the exit, to the craft shop and small refreshment bar at the back, where you'll find the most delicious *pisang goreng* or fried bananas.

Then drive back to the waterside and turn right past the ornate, white Abu Bakar Mosque and carry on for a km or so until you see a great Japanese style palace high on your right.

At the sign for **Istana Bukit Serene**, turn right and almost immediately left in front of the Kebun Bunga Istana, or palace nursery, to the corner of Jalan Tahar to **Crafttown.**

There you can visit a batik factory and watch delicate flowers being hand-drawn in beeswax using a *chanting*, a metal holder with a spout. The outline is then coloured in on the dyed cloth. The process is fascinating, and the products beautiful, a wide selection being available in the adjoining shop.

Then go back and up the hill to admire the view from the top outside the Istana Bukit Serene, the present home of the Sultan of Johor. You'll probably be ready for lunch now, so drive back along Jalan Skudai until you see a sign for **Jaws 5** on your left. Turn in, and enjoy the rustic atmosphere, glorious view and excellent food. It's peaceful just

looking out over the Straits at the *kelong*s or fishing traps, to which fish are lured with bright lights at night.

After lunch drive on down Jalan Abu Bakar and turn left just before you reach the mosque, **Masjid Abu Bakar**. Walk around the grounds. Unfortunately, tourists in the past have not respected the sanctity of the place, and nowadays non-Muslims are no longer allowed inside. The building is beautiful outside though, and there's plenty of life, with vendors of prayer mats, paintings and curry puffs.

Leave by the green arch on the other side and bear left up the hill on Jalan Gertak Merah and then left into Jalan Datuk Menteri and you will come to the **Muslim Cemetery and Mausoleum**. The latter is usually closed, but you can drive up to the lovely yellow building and look at the graves. All point to Mecca, and the stones, one at the head and one at the foot of the uncremated body, indicate by their shape whether a man or woman lies there. The round stones are for men, the flat ones for the women.

On leaving, turn left and then left again into Jalan Mahmudiah and then right down Jalan Cik Besar Zubaidah. Now you're in a Malay *kampong* or village, so watch for the chickens, and see how many different fruit trees you can spot. The houses are on stilts and are surrounded by flowering plants and trees bearing mangos, star-fruit, jackfruit and bananas. Some people grow sugar cane and keep monkeys and birds in cages.

It's a relaxed lifestyle, and at 6B, you may be invited in by Ungku

Singapore from the opposite shore

Adleen Ungku Abu Bakar to become part of the family. Take your shoes off and look around.

After browsing at the little stalls selling pretty souvenirs, retrace your steps up along Jalan Mahmudiah, and turn right past the whole of the cemetery and follow the road as it turns sharply right. On your left is a football field (it's the national sport) and on the next corner is a sign for **JARO** where you turn right to the **Johor Area Rehabilitation Organisation**.

This is a rehabilitation centre where all kinds of beautiful handicrafts made by physically handicapped and chronically ill people are sold. Go downstairs and watch books being bound in fine leather and baskets of all shapes and sizes being made. Then go upstairs again and spend your last Ringgit, it's all in a good cause and you'll have wonderful souvenirs of Malaysia. The Coffee House has tea, coffee, cold drinks and good cake too.

After that it will be time to wend your way back to the hurly burly of Singapore, after a glimpse of a slower, calmer side of Asia.

2. Desaru

A perfect picnic spot.

About 2 hour's drive from Singapore, on the south eastern tip of Peninsular Malaysia lies the lovely **Desaru Beach**. White sands fringed by casuarina trees offer Singaporeans and visitors to the region a chance to get away from it all. Even at weekends, when the hotels are full, and the patches of beach in front of them are crowded, you can still stroll along the water's edge in solitude.

If you are driving, follow the signs to Desaru and Mersing through **Johor Baru** and drive through plantations of rubber and oil palms to **Kota Tinggi**. There you can have a break looking at the waterfalls.

Then continue the journey, keeping your eyes open for the signs. You'll soon find yourself on the long straight road which you follow until you eventually turn left to Desaru. Watch out for monkeys which sometimes play by the roadside.

The easiest way to arrange a visit to Desaru is to book in Singapore for **The Desaru View Hotel** by calling 250-3155. Then a two-way transfer by coach can be arranged for S$45. All the hotel rooms face the sea, and cost S$135, or S$165 for Saturday nights inclusive of an American breakfast. There you can relax by the pool, play tennis and hire bikes and explore the coast. There is also an 18-hole golf course. The hotel is very popular with Japanese tourists, so the Japanese restaurant is good, and the karaoke lounge popular.

Picnics on the beach are fun, but the currents here are notorious. So take care when swimming. The sea air is invigorating, especially after the humidity of Singapore. Even when it rains, it's balmy, so you'll enjoy this unspoilt corner of Malaysia whatever time of year you visit.

3. The Island of Batam in Indonesia

Sun, sand and sea in the tropical paradise of Turi Beach.

Within sight of Singapore, but worlds away, is the Indonesian Island of **Batam**. Two-thirds the size of Singapore, and just 20 km (13 miles) away, Batam is one of the 3,000 islands of the Rhiau Archipelago.

Oil, minerals and forestry have long made the island an important industrial centre, but in recent years Batam has turned to the tourist market. New hotels have sprung up and there is now a regular ferry service between **Finger Pier** in Singapore and Sekupang Ferry Point in Batam.

The journey itself lasts only half an hour, but immigration and waiting time, plus transfer to a hotel makes it all up to about 2 hours. However, going over, you gain an hour, as Indonesian time is one hour behind Singapore.

Of all the hotels, the loveliest is the **Turi Beach Resort**, a cluster of Balinese-styled cottages nestled on a hillside sloping to the sea.

The Singapore Office on 732-2577 or fax 733-3740 will arrange the hotel booking, ferry and transfer to Turi Beach for you. The rate for a standard room is US$85 for single occupancy, US$95 for double, with a deluxe suite for two costing US$200. There's a 20 percent surcharge at weekends and on the eve of public holidays.

Packages can be arranged to include travel and breakfast, with prices starting from S$150 per person for one night in a twin room.

When you arrive at the spacious entrance hall of the hotel, you will have a glorious view across the South China Sea to the distant highrise buildings of Singapore, where you can just make out the Airport Tower. You'll then be taken to your chalet in a small cart, as the beautifully landscaped grounds are so extensive and steep.

A palm frond roof above, a balcony overlooking the sea, a fridge full of cold drinks, what more could you ask for? Perhaps a wonderful pool under the palms, restaurants serving delicious seafood, shops with Indonesian arts and crafts, tennis, T.V., windsurfers, jet scooters and bicycles ... well, they're all here. So just relax and let the gentle Indonesians look after you as only they know how.

When you reluctantly tear yourself away from the island, you can drown your sorrows Duty Free.

Friendly service at Turi Beach Resort

Dining E

Wherever you go in Singapore, you can be sure of finding something to eat, and it's usually delicious. Eating is the national pastime, and from hawker stall to plush hotel, from *nouvelle cuisine* to exotic Thai dishes, the gamut of choice is yours.

Most hotels have several restaurants, with coffee shops staying open longest and serving the greatest variety of different food, and the more specialised restaurants offering one particular cuisine. Although these are easy to find, the choice is confusing so I am including some great favourites. I have also suggested more interesting venues off the beaten track.

Singapore's ethnic mix and the people's love of food ensures that Chinese, Malay and Indian food is readily available. Restaurants offering food from all over the world seem to have opened up in competition. Prices range from unbelievably low at the stalls to staggeringly high in the top class restaurants.

"Chinese food please." says the tourist, only to be asked, "What kind?" For here we never simply refer to Chinese food. There are as many as 80 different styles of cooking, although in general we tend to think in terms of four or five main regions of China.

Stir-fry is essentially Cantonese, perhaps the cuisine best known in the west. Freshness of ingredients is of paramount importance,

Hot stuff at the Satay Club

and the flavouring is subtle and mild. Not so often available else-where is the fascinating array of small delicacies served from bamboo baskets which make up dim sum.

From the north comes the famed Peking Duck, a must for the gourmet, and the Mongolian influence has resulted in "drunken" dishes, cooked in wine, with dumplings and wheat being used as the staple rather than rice.

Hainanese Chicken Rice is a perennial favourite – succulent chicken meat sliced on top of cucumber, served with rice cooked in the stock, broth and three sauces: soy, chilli and ground ginger and garlic.

The delicate flavour and careful cooking of the Teochews will appeal to purists, and for a long lasting, sociable meal like an Asian *fondue*, try steamboat, where you cook your own seafood, meat and vegetables in a pot of boiling broth.

Taiwanese porridges, Hakka stuffed bean curd dishes, Hokkien fried mee and *popiah* or spring rolls are other favourites from other regions.

But for the lover of all things hot and spicy, the sensational Szechuan cuisine is beyond compare. Prawns with dried chilli and the hot and sour soup are less a taste, more an experience.

91

The blending of pungent spices is the hallmark of Indian food and there is a range of choice, from mild *tandoori* dishes to mind-blowing *vindaloo* curries. The Moghul influence is evident in the northern use of a clay oven. Wheat replaces rice as the staple, in the form of oven-baked *naan*. Many south Indian restaurants cater for vegetarians. Little India abounds with restaurants of all regional foods.

The most famous of Malay delicacies is *satay*, small pieces of marinated meat on bamboo sticks barbequed and served with a succulent peanut sauce, and *ketupat* or compressed rice. Like much Malay food, the dish probably originated in Indonesia, and the two cuisines have much in common. The food is delicately spiced. *Nasi padang* is a choice of spiced dishes served with rice; *gado-gado* is an unusual salad of steamed or raw vegetables, fried beancurd and potatoes with peanut sauce and garnished with deep fried *belinjau* nut chips. Other favourites include *nasi goreng* (fried rice), *soto ayam* (chicken broth with bean sprouts) and beef *rendang* (spiced coconut beef stew).

But what of Singapore itself? The nearest thing to indigenous cuisine is really a mix of the influences of Chinese, Malay and Indonesian as developed by Straits-born Chinese, and called *Nonya* cuisine. *Popiah* (spring rolls), *laksa lemak* (rice noodles in a coconut soup) and the distinctive taste of *blacan*, prawn paste, are some of the delicious results of this combination.

The waters around Singapore ensure fresh supplies of seafood and excellent local fish such as *ikan merah* and pomfret, and there are

many places where the catch is cooked well. One of Singapore's all-time favourites, and perhaps even the national dish, is chilli crab. Using a hammer and your fingers, making a mess of yourself and the table; chilli crabs are an unforgettable culinary experience. Another contender for the national dish title is the hot and spicy fish head curry, originally Indian and now often cooked in Chinese or Malay style.

Japanese raw fish called *sushi*, and *teppanyaki* cooked in front of you on a hot table and other dishes have become firm favourites here too. Then there are those who say that of all the different styles of cooking in the region, the one which gives you the best of all worlds is Thai, with the subtle taste of lemon grass and mint, the fiery soup, *tom yang kung* and wonderful ways of cooking fresh fish and vegetables.

In Singapore, western food from the Americas to Europe is of a high standard, but when in Asia, why not eat Asia

Where To Go

As a rough indication of how much you can expect to pay, the following signs indicate the price of an average meal for one person without wine or drinks. Of course, the price is very much dependent on what you order, if you insist on sharks' fin, abalone, suckling pig etc. in a Chinese restaurant, or *pate de foie gras* and a dozen oysters when eating western, the guide may appear somewhat inaccurate!

Very Expensive	****	**S$50 and above**
Expensive	***	**S$30 - S$50**
Moderate	**	**S$15 - S$30**
Reasonable	*	**S$15 and below**

Chinese Style

Cantonese
***

Shang Palace Restaurant, Shangri-La Hotel. Tel: 737-3644
Chinese courtyard setting for dim sum at lunchtime and a wide range of a la carte choices in the evening. Try sharks' fin soup with crab meat and minced pigeon wrapped in lettuce.

****

**Hai Tien Lo Chinese Restaurant, The Pan Pacific Hotel.
Tel: 336-8111**
Extensive menu and views.

**

Lei Garden Restaurant, Boulevard Hotel. Tel: 235-8122
Highly recommended, especially for Peking duck and lobster.

A glass of herb tea ?

***

Wah Lok Restaurant, Carlton Hotel. Tel: 337-3193
Dim sum is very popular here, combined with extensive a la carte dishes.

**

Mitzi Cantonese Restaurant, 24/26 Murray Street. Tel: 222-8281
Recommended by discerning locals.

**

126 Eating House, 126 Sims Avenue. Tel: 746-4757
A popular place for a wide selection of Hong Kong dim sum dishes.

Szechuan
***

**Dragon City, Novotel Orchid Inn, (214 Dunearn Road).
Tel: 254-7070/254-5477**
One of the most popular restaurants in Singapore, don't forget to book.

***

Min Jiang, Goodwood Park Hotel. Tel: 737-7411 ext. 1704

Teochew
**

Ban Seng, 79 New Bridge Road. Tel: 533-1471
The original Teochew restaurant in Singapore, which has changed little.

***

House of Blossoms, Marina Mandarin Hotel. Tel: 338-3388
Rich decor and beautifully-presented dishes.

Northern - Beijing
****

**Prima Tower Revolving Restaurant, 201 Keppel Road.
Tel: 222-8822**
It takes almost two hours for a complete revolution, so enjoy a spectacular view of the port as you eat.

Hokkien
**

**Beng Hiang, Murray Street, Food Alley, off Maxwell Road.
Tel: 221-6684**

Hunan
***

**Charming Garden, Novotel Orchid Inn, 214 Dunearn Road.
Tel: 251-8149**
Overlooking a little pool and garden, the restaurant is popular. Try steamed red tilapia, a delicate fish, with crispy soya bean crumb topping.

Mixed
**

**Westlake Eating House, Blk. 4 #02-139 Queen's Road.
Tel: 474-7283**
Located in a housing estate, this restaurant is popular with locals and expatriates alike, and you can choose dishes from all over China.

Vegetarian

**

Miao Yi Vegetarian Restaurant, #03-01/02 Coronation Shopping Plaza. Tel: 467-1331
A boon for the vegetarian who loves local flavours.

Indian

Northern
**

**Moti Mahal, 18 Murray Street, Food Alley, off Maxwell Road.
Tel: 221-4338**
Considered by many to be the best Indian restaurant in South East Asia.

**

**Orchard Maharajah, 25 Cuppage Road, Cuppage Terrace.
Tel: 732-6331**
Delightful decor and cuisine.

Punjabi
*

**Ujagar Singh's, 7 St. Gregory's Place, off Hill Street.
Tel: 336-1586**
Totally unpretentious room upstairs serving superb food at such low
prices that you can afford a wide selection.

South and Vegetarian
**

**Annalakshmi, Excelsior Hotel, #02-10, 5 Coleman Street.
Tel: 339-9993**
Wonderful setting for exquisite cuisine.

*

Komala Vilas, 76-78 Serangoon Road. Tel: 293-6980
In the heart of Little India, simple but good.

*

**Bombay Woodlands, B1-06 Forum Galleria (next to Hilton Hotel)
Tel: 235-2712**
Clean, calm restaurant in the middle of the shopping district, serving
very good vegetarian food.

Malay

***

Aziza's, 36 Emerald Hill Road. Tel: 235-1130
Friendly service, cosy *kampong* atmosphere and good, mildly-spiced food.

Aziza's

Indonesian

*

Sanur, #04-17/18 Centrepoint. Tel: 734-2192
Very popular and invariably crowded. Best reserve a table.

Local

**

Spices Oriental Brasserie, #05-14/27 Shaw Centre. Tel: 235-9393
A centrally-located restaurant with delightful coffeeshop ambience and decor as well as an excellent range of local food. Some of the dishes are displayed so that you can ask questions and make your choice.

*

Our Makan Shop, 74 Race Course Road. Tel: 292-9475
Indian and Malay dishes served in a simple setting.

Nonya

Ψ

Nonya and Baba Restaurant, 262-264 River Valley Road. Tel: 734-1382
Traditional setting for wonderful, authentic *nonya* dishes.

Seafood

**

Long Beach, 610 Bedok Road. Tel: 445-8833
Evenings only, for some of the best chilli crab in town; the pepper crabs are delicious too but not for the faint-hearted.

**

Ng Tiong Choon, Sembawang Fishing Pond and Seafood Village, 59 Lorong Chuntum (off Lorong Gambas). Tel: 754-1991/257-7939
Off Mandai Road, you can reach the restaurant by taxi or MRT to Yishun, then shuttle bus at 9.05 and 10.45 a.m., and 2.45, 4.30 and 7.15 p.m. Bus No. 171 or 137 drops you at the main road, then you walk. Right out in the countryside, overlooking the ponds, you sit outdoors to eat good seafood and local fare.

**

Palm Beach Seafood Restaurant, National Stadium, Kallang. Tel: 344-3088
A huge place, and firm favourite with locals who queue up for the chilli and pepper crabs and crispy *yu cha kuay* seafood rolls.

Japanese

****

Keyaki, Pan Pacific Hotel. Tel: 336-8111
A lovely water garden leads to the restaurant where excellent Japanese food, including *teppanyaki*, is served.

Thai

***

Chao Phaya Seafood Market and Restaurant, Blk. 730 #02-4272, Ang Mo Kio Ave. 6. Tel: 456-0118
In the evening you choose your ingredients raw and select the way you'd like them cooked. At lunchtime there is a varied menu.

***

Bangkok Garden Thai Restaurant, Hotel Negara. (Next to Orchard Towers). Tel: 737-0811
A firm favourite of the *aficionado*s.

Eastern and Western

****

The Pinnacle, Raffles Place, 60th Floor, OUB Centre. Tel: 532-2166
East meets west high above the river.

****

Compass Rose Restaurant, Westin Stamford Hotel. Tel: 338-8585.

Spectacular vista with delicate decor and cuisine blending Asian and western flavours.

If you can't make up your mind, **Food Alley, off Murray Street,** is a road full of restaurants of all kinds, a delightful place to wander along while you decide what to eat and where.

Last but certainly not least, are the many food centres, some outside, some in airconditioned buildings and shopping centres, where the hawkers produce delicious food at low, low prices. These places are to be found all over town, because this is how the locals eat. You can try all kinds of food, and watch it being cooked. Just place your order and indicate where you are sitting and whatever you want to try will be brought to you. There's no better way to sample a wide range of local delicacies, and there's no better value for money.

The most famous is **Newton Circus**, and the prettiest, the **Satay Club** down on Queen Elizabeth Walk, where you can dine under the stars.

Continental

****

Latour, Shangri-La Hotel. Tel: 737-3644
Exquisite cuisine, souffles for pudding are a speciality, and the lunchtime buffet is the best in town.

****

Le Duc, Omni Marco Polo Hotel. Tel: 474-7141
Romantic elegance and superb cuisine, especially the pressed duck.

*** _****

Casablanca, 7 Emerald Hill Road. Tel: 235-9328
Wine and dine extremely well in an atmosphere of romantic nostalgia.

***

The Flying Dutchman, 10A Duxton Hill. Tel: 227-9630
Old Chinese shophouse converted nautical style into captain's room and upper deck, serving delicious Dutch and continental cuisine.

*** _ ****

Oscar's Brasserie and Wine Bar, 30 Robinson Road. Tel: 223-4033
Attractive black, white and red decor with walls full of modern prints gives an informal atmosphere. Expertly prepared light, brasserie-type dishes. Popular with executives for "Lunch on the Hop" and "Apres le Grind".

French

****
Maxim's de Paris, Regent Singapore Hotel. Tel: 733-8888
Yes, it's here too!

***
La Grande Bouffe, 53/55 Sunset Way. Tel: 467-6847
This delightful little restaurant is out in the suburbs but you'll eat well and easily make up the taxi fare by the savings on the extensive yet extremely reasonable wine list.

*** - ****
La Brasserie, Marco Polo Hotel. Tel: 474-7141
Everyone's favourite.

English

**
"Upstairs" English Restaurant, Tudor Court, 145A Tanglin Road. Tel: 732-3811
Cosy English setting for traditional fare.

American

****
Nutmegs, Hyatt Regency Hotel. Tel: 733-1188
Black and white art deco; interesting menu and delicious dessert buffet.

**
Hard Rock Cafe, 50 Cuscaden Road. Tel: 235-5232
Quick, delightful service as you freak out to the great sounds.

Italian

*** - ****
Ristorante Bologna, Marina Mandarin Hotel. Tel: 338-3388
Overlooking a waterfall, with a lively band to entertain you as you tuck into Italian specialities.

**

Pete's Place, basement, Hyatt Regency Hotel. Tel: 733-1188
Family favourite with extensive salad bar and plenty of pizza and pasta.

***

Prego's, Level 3, The Westin Plaza. Tel: 338-8585
Connoisseur's choice for pasta and all the other Italian delights.

Mexican

**

El Felipe's, 13 Lorong Mambong, Holland Village. Tel: 468-1520
Popular venue for Mexican favourites.

* - **

Margarita's, 108 Faber Drive, off Jalan Lempeng. Tel: 777-1782
Off the beaten track in Clementi, try the namesake cocktail and tuck into *taco*s, *nacho*s, *enchilada*s and more.

International

****

Trader Vic's, Level 5, Hotel New Otani. Tel: 337-2249
People come to this place for the Polynesian atmosphere and the tropical tipples, but the exotic food is just as good.

The undecided should make their way to **Marina Village** (see Nightlife) where you can wander around a dozen restaurants, enjoying drinks in 6 pubs while you make up your mind what and where to eat.

What To Drink

All this food needs something to wash it down with, and the world-famous locally brewed beers, Tiger and Anchor, are excellent accompaniment to Asian food. At Chinese banquets cognac is often drunk with a meal, or Chinese tea, which is almost always served free of charge. Wines and spirits of all kinds are usually available, with longer lists in restaurants serving western cuisine.

You really shouldn't leave Singapore without trying a "Singapore Sling", an irresistible mixture of gin, Peter Heering, Benedictine, Cointreau, Angostura Bitter, pineapple juice and fresh lime, decorated with fresh pineapple and a cherry. Cheers!

Shopping

"Shop 'til you drop" they say here, and indeed that is a temptation. From the shiny new shopping centres to the musty, old shophouses of Chinatown, there is a selection of merchandise possibly unrivalled in the world. Goods imported from all over the globe vie with locally-made bargains. The main problems are where to start, and when to stop.

The Singapore Tourist Promotion Board has authorised certain shops to display a red Merlion sticker as a symbol of its recommendation. However, if you do have any complaints, the Consumer Association of Singapore (CASE, Tel: 222-4165) is there to help.

The shopping centres which have sprung up over the last ten years or so house small shops as well as department stores. The former are staffed by keen salesmen, ready to explain anything and eager for custom; the latter by less than enthusiastic shopgirls, so you can browse for hours unnoticed.

Bargain only in the smaller shops, and let the salesperson know if you intend to pay by credit card, as he will have to allow for the surcharge. If you have bargained for a while and agreed on a price, you are under a moral obligation to buy!

Antique hunting

What to Buy

Cameras and Audio Equipment

Despite the currently strong Singapore dollar, prices here remain attractive, particularly for photographic equipment and the latest walkman or portable CD player. CDs and tapes are often cheaper here than elsewhere.

It's a good idea to get an international guarantee, but if you want to risk directly imported goods intended just for the local market, you can save on the price. If you don't see what you want in the shop, ask, because it can be fetched for you in no time.

Computer Equipment

Everything for the computer buff, local and imported, from the latest laptop to a stunning selection of software. Don't forget to check the voltage.

Watches and Jewellery

Singapore glitters, and it is likely to be with gold, probably the very pure 22 and 24 K yellow Chinese gold. But it's more than jewellery, it's an investment, for you can trade it in for cash at the current gold price.

Watches are sold tax-free, and the choice is never-ending, from a lifetime's investment in a Rolex to a cheap plastic fun watch.

The selection of jewellery here is mind-boggling. Chinese love jade, and from the paler Nephrite to the bright green Jadite, all kinds of pretty pendants, rings and earrings are made. Lovely statues are sculpted in jade, often of Chinese deities. These are also carved in ivory or whalebone. Ivory trade is now banned worldwide so be careful in case you cannot bring purchases into your country.

Live orchid blooms coated with pure 22K gold to preserve their beauty, can be worn as rings, earrings, pendants or bracelets.

Softly shining Mikimoto pearls from Japan are laid out row upon row, and freshwater pearls of all colours are cheap enough for you to buy several strands to twist into a collar. Indian jewellers sell intricate pieces in bright gold. You can choose a gemstone and make up your own design, or rely on the expertise of the greatest designers of jewellery in the world, such as Cartier and Bvlgari.

Fashion

Designer shops are everywhere for the fashion conscious, but you can always have that special dress copied, or a suit made to measure by one of the many tailors.

There is lovely *batik* from Malaysia and Indonesia as well as locally

For the fashion conscious

printed *batik* with orchid motifs on soft cotton. You can find silks from China, Thailand, India and Malaysia.

What about a pair of shoes to go with the new outfit? There's the whole range from Jourdan to attractive locally made footwear which look great, even though they may not last as long as imports. You'll find handbags and belts of all shapes, sizes and prices too.

Goods made from alligator, crocodile and snake skins are good buys, but check with your embassy in case there is an import ban in your country.

Antiques and Asian Exotica

As Singapore is a trading port in the heart of Asia, the selection of fascinating and sometimes quite extraordinary artefacts from Bangkok to Borneo and beyond is one of many boons for the shopper.

You can find baskets and lovely shell dishes and lamps from the Philippines. From Japan come miniature masterpieces of design, tiny sewing or writing compacts the size of a credit card, as well as lacquer ware and delicate porcelain. What about silk photoframes, ties and jackets from Thailand, Indian *papier mâché* and brass ware, and sandlewood carvings and gems from Sri Lanka? Then there's a whole range of items in Selangor Pewter from Malaysia, and Buddhas from Burma and Thailand. If you can't carry it all, then ship it in a Korean or camphorwood chest.

For the connoisseur, prints and maps as well as old editions of books on the region can be found, and also old porcelain, figurines and coins.

A certificate of antiquity will be given with a genuine antique purchase.

Oriental Carpets

In Singapore you will find an enormous selection of beautiful Oriental carpets, from tribal rugs to exquisite silk on silk carpets with glorious colours and intricate designs. When buying, look at the workmanship: the dying, knotting and clipping in the finished carpet. The more knots per square cm, the finer (and more expensive) the carpet, so turn it over and have a look at the back. Buy what you will be happy with, but beware of being charged for an antique piece unless that is what you really want. Take the carpet into daylight to see the colours, and take your time to choose. Just remember, it won't be fault free, as only Allah is perfect!

Things Chinese

Unbreakable but beautiful is the colourful cloisonne ware from China, made into everything from pens and earrings to lampstands. Exquisite lace table linen, whether as cloths or mats look elegant for dinner parties. Embroidered Mandarin sleeves, old and new, look wonderful framed, or set under the glass of a coffee table.

China produces china too – ceramics, old, new and repro' for display or daily use can be found. Paper lamps, fans, carvings and silk paintings are pretty and easy to transport home.

Where to Buy It

If it's shopping in Singapore, it has to be Orchard Road, so we'll start there. Right at the top end, actually in Tanglin Road, is the lovely **Tudor Court**, full of designer shops, from Ken Done to Kritzia.

Carpets for sale

Walking on down towards Orchard Road proper, you come to my favourite haunt, the **Tanglin Shopping Centre**. Down in the basement on your right is **Design Thai** where you'll find a wonderful selection of clothes in Thai silk and cotton, and pretty boxes, bags and photoframes made up in these glorious, colourful fabrics. Up on the next level is **C.T. Hoo**, who have the widest selection of pearls in Singapore. **Hassan's Carpet** is just along the corridor.

A remarkable range of antique prints, old maps and rare books can be found in **Antiques of the Orient** on level 2, and an excellent choice of modern books on the region in **Select Books** on the next floor. Browse around and you'll find fascinating artefacts from all over Asia, jewellery shops, shoe shops and plenty of places for refreshment if the shopping gets tiring. Either cross the road and explore the little shops opposite, or go straight on to Bangkok's famous **Jim Thomson's** at the Orchard Parade Hotel from where you can cross over to the **Delphi Building** for wonderful clothes and English porcelain.

Orchard Towers beckons with jewellery and silk, antiques and shoes. Don't miss one of the cheapest and best selections of electronic equipment, cameras, watches and binoculars down in the basement at **Electronic Towers**. **Palais Renaissance** with exquisite boutiques is next door.

If you need to appease peevish infants, cross over to Toys R' Us, the world's largest toy store chain in Forum Galleria. Below the highrise pagoda of the Dynasty Hotel is **Tangs**, where you can buy almost anythings. Don't miss the baskets, china and appliances in the basement. **Lucky Plaza** next door is for the camera and watch enthusiast. Wander on down past the fashion paradise of the **Promenade** and the **Paragon** and past **Esprit** and you'll eventually reach **Centrepoint**. This is home to Britain's Marks and Spencer, as

In the heart of Orchard Road

well as Singapore's original department store **Robinson's** and a host of other shops, including The Body Shop, Mondi, Mothercare and Bruno Magli. On the second floor Sunny and Grace has a colourful selection of exotic cotton and silk clothes.

Outside the Orchard Road area, **People's Park Complex** in Chinatown offers bales and bales of all kinds of fabric. Bargain hard, you might just end up with the lowest-priced fabrics in town. **Pidemco Centre** not far away is the place for local gold and jewellery.

The **Funan Centre** in Hill Street and **Sim Lim Square** in Rochor Road are full of electronic appliances and computers of all shapes and sizes. Explanations are readily forthcoming if you aren't an expert.

If you would like a bag or wallet made to your own design, head for **Chan Yew** in Prinsep Street, where you'll also find a selection of goods in leather and crocodile skin at the best prices in town.

Holland Shopping Centre in **Holland Village**, a little further out of town, is the expat ladies' haunt, and you'll find a wide range of bags, shoes, jewellery and clothes from batik to comfortable casuals at Coretti. All your gift and souvenir problems will be solved in **Lim's Arts and Crafts**, a real oriental treasure trove.

The Great Blue Dive Shop sells everything for divers, as well as offering to arrange diving trips and courses.

Go down Lorong Liput and explore **Lorong Mambong** behind the shopping centre for baskets, porcelain and antiques.

Just along Holland Road at Jalan Jelita is **Jelita Cold Storage**, where **Renee Hoy Fine Arts**, open from 10 a.m. to 7 p.m., is a must. Exquisite Asian treasures fill the shop, and any questions you ask will be patiently answered, or if you prefer, you can browse undisturbed for as long as you like. **Jessica Art N' Craft** is next door, another lovely Oriental boutique to explore. For furniture, antiques and cone the shops in Watten Estate along Bukit Timah are a must.

Arab Street, off Beach Road, is another great place for baskets, batik and all things Islamic, **Serangoon Road** for goods from the Subcontinent, and of course **Chinatown** for souvenirs of every kind from paper umbrellas to ginseng.

This just gives you the tip of the monumental iceberg of shopping possibilities in Singapore. The hotel arcades are enticing and shopping centres spring up like mushrooms, so do explore, and if you are looking for something in particular, use the *Singapore Buying Guide* directory.

Shops open at about 10 a.m. and many stay that way until 9 p.m. which gives you plenty of time to spend your money.

Renee Hoy Fine Arts Private Limited

The Home of Collector's Classics

Calendar of Special Events

In multi-racial and multi-religious Singapore, festivals and celebrations are held all through the year. Join in.

Dates here apply to 1991 only. Festivals that follow the lunar calendar sometimes have no dates as they have not yet been confirmed. Check the calendar at the time of your visit.

January/February

The Christian **New Year's Day** starts the year on **January 1**, and is followed about a month later by **Chinese New Year** on **February 15 and 16**, which is fixed in accordance with the lunar calendar.

During February, Singapore is decked out in red and gold, pussy willow and mandarin trees are sold and gifts of oranges and money in special *hong bao* envelopes are given, all accompanied by the drumming and prancing of the lion dancers. A Chingay parade is held and the streets of Chinatown are brightly lit and thronged with people buying and selling traditional decorations and delicacies.

Before Chinese New Year the Indian harvest festival of **Ponggal** is held, where a new pot of rice is

allowed to boil over to symbolise prosperity, and food is offered to the gods in the Sri Perumal Temple in Serangoon Road.

Then comes the startling Indian festival of **Thaipusam**. Devotees carry enormous arched structures called *kavadis* for about 3 km (2 miles), from the Sri Perumal Temple to the Chettiar Temple in Tank Road in gratitude or supplication to Lord Murugan. The *kavadis* are decorated with peacock feathers and are held in place by hooks and skewers which pierce the body. No blood is drawn by this as the faithful have prepared themselves for the ordeal with prayer and fasting.

Twice a year, in February and October, Chinese mediums in a trance and a jerking sedan chair announce the **Birthday of the Monkey God**, which is celebrated at the Monkey God Temple in Seng Poh Road.

March/April

The muslim fasting month of **Ramadan** falls between March and April, when believers eat special food after dusk, consuming nothing in daylight hours until the celebration feast of **Hari Raya Puasa** or Hari Raya Aidil Fitri on **April 16.** Then Geylang is decorated and lit up and families gather after the sighting of the new moon.

Also around this time is **Qing Ming**, when the Chinese honour their ancestors, burning incense papers, hell money and paper gifts on the graves of their forebears which are tidied for the occasion.

May/June

Vesak Day on **May 28** commemorates the Buddha's birth, enlightenment and entry into Nirvana, and prayer and meditation are followed by the release of caged birds.

Ritual celebrations for the **Birthday of the Third Prince**, a child god, are held in Chinese temples in May, with mediums in trance cutting themselves with swords and smearing the blood onto paper for devotees.

The **Dragon Boat Festival** on **June 16** sees dragon dances and exciting races between crews from all around the world paddling traditional craft across Marina Bay. It is held in remembrance of the poet Qu Yuan who drowned himself in protest against political corruption, and fishermen beat drums and their paddles on the water to try to save him from being eaten by fish.

August/September

August is an important month.

National Day Military Parade

To celebrate **National Day** on **August 9**, activities abound, such as the Singapore River Regatta and a food-and-fair bazaar at the Marina Promenade.

Then it's the **Chinese Hungry Ghost Month** which lasts from **August 8 - September 7** this year, when the gates of hell are opened and the ghosts visit this world. Incense sticks and hell money are burned and food is offered to placate the ghosts, but no Chinese would marry during this period.

The wonderful autumn moon is celebrated by the Chinese by giving children brightly coloured lanterns which are lit from within by candles. The **Mooncake Festival, September 22**, brings delicious moon shaped pastries with fillings of red bean paste, nuts or preserved duck eggs.

Chettiar Temple

A lantern display from China lights up the Chinese Gardens for the month.

October

In October, Indian temples then become the venue for classical dance and musical performances in honour of Dhurga, Lakshmi and Saraswathi, the consorts of the Hindu Trinity for the **Festival of Navrathri**.

The **Thimithi Festival** is on **October 27**. Fire walking in honour of the goddess Draupadi, heroine of the *Mahabharata* epic, who walked on fire to prove her chastity, takes place in the Sri Mariamman Temple in South Bridge Road.

Kusu Island is the destination for Chinese and Muslim Pilgrims from **mid October to mid November**. According to legend two fishermen were carried to safety on the island on the back of a giant turtle which rescued them after their boat sank. Of different faiths, the one built the Tua Pekong Taoist Temple, the other the Keramat hilltop shrine.

The **Festival of the Nine Emperor Gods**, during which they are said to cure all ills and grant good fortune on their nine-day visit to earth, is celebrated from **October 8 - 16** with *wayangs* (Chinese operas) and a great procession with the effigies of the gods borne aloft in sedan chairs.

November/December

Little India glows with gentle lights and garlands in celebration of **Deepavali**, when light triumphs over darkness. **November 5**.

Singapore then lights up (usually in Orchard Road) for **Christmas**, on **December 25**, and the year winds up with carol singing in the streets and parties everywhere.

Community Week, the **Youth Festival**, **Film** and **Arts Festivals** and cultural months for the main racial groups add to the total of events. As if all that were not enough, Singapore has invented its own **Merlion Week**, seven days of fun for Singaporeans and visitors alike, held mid year. The calendar is full, there's always something interesting going on somewhere.

What to Know:
Practical Information

TRAVEL ESSENTIALS

Climate/When to Visit

The average daily temperature is 26.6°C (80°F), often rising to around 30°C (87°F) in the heat of the day, and cooling only to around 23°C (75°F) at night. Humidity varies between 64 and 96 percent.

The Northeast Monsoon blows from December to March, and the Southwest from June to September making it breezier during these months. Spectacular thunderstorms occur frequently between the monsoons, in April and May, and October and November. The average rainfall is 237 cm (93 inches).

The slightly cooler rainy season lasts roughly from November to January, winter time in Europe, North America and Japan, and the long tropical days here are especially welcome to travellers from these countries then. The heavens are prone to open suddenly to drench everything and everyone, often causing traffic jams, and making it harder to hail a taxi by the road. But it's usually all over quickly, leaving lush smelling vegetation and steaming pavements sparkling in the sunlight.

June and July are often extremely hot, more conducive to lying at the poolside or browsing in the airconditioned shopping centres than to sightseeing.

Getting There

By Air
Landing in Singapore's Changi Airtropolis is a luxurious experience. Even without the newly-opened Terminal 2 this was the world's best airport, and now the two terminals share the load of increasing passenger and air traffic. All major airlines land here, baggage handling is quick and taxis queue up to whisk arriving passengers to their hotels.

Finger Pier Container Port

By Sea

More and more cruise liners are stopping off at Singapore, sailing in from Europe, Hong Kong, America and India to what is now the busiest port in the world.

Overland

There are good roads into Singapore through Malaysia, from Ipoh and Kuala Lumpur on the west coast, and Kota Bahru on the east.

A railway links Singapore to Kuala Lumpur (K.L.) and Bangkok, with daily trains leaving Bangkok at 3.15 p.m. and arriving in K.L. at 8.15 p.m. the following night. From K.L. departure time is 10 p.m. and you eventually arrive in Singapore at 7 a.m. the next morning. 1st Class fare from Bangkok is S$237.80 and about S$50 from K.L. Further details are available from the Railway Station at Keppel Road, Tel: 222-5165.

Visas

As long as you have a valid passport, onward travel reservations and adequate finance, you do not need a visa to enter Singapore. However, citizens of China, India and the USSR are required to produce a visa. You will normally be given a two-week tourist visa, so remember to check the date and renew if necessary at the Immigration Office, Pidemco Centre (Tel: 532-2877).

Vaccination

A smallpox vaccination is necessary if you are arriving from an infected country.

Money Matters

The Singapore Dollar is currently at about S$1.75 to the US$ and S$3.3 to the Pound Sterling, as is the Brunei dollar which is also valid currency here. The Malaysian dollar is valued rather lower. There are no restrictions on the amount of currency you can bring in to the country. Banks and licensed money changers offer better rates than hotels and you are never far from one or the other. Major credit cards are widely accepted.

What to Wear

Casual clothes are comfortable in the heat, and although many hotels are very cool inside. Shorts are quite acceptable in most places.

Ties are only worn for formal occasions, and jackets almost never, although some clubs and discos do have a strict dress code.

Electricity

Electrical supply is on a 220-240 volt, 50 Hz system. Most hotels have transformers for 110-120 volt, 60 Hz appliances.

Airport Tax

A charge of S$12 for passengers departing overseas, and S$5 for those going to Malaysia and Brunei, are levied at the airport. It is possible to buy these coupons at most hotels.

GETTING ACQUAINTED

Geography

The Republic of Singapore consists of the main island, about 616 sq km (238 sq miles) in area, and 58 other islets. Located at the southern tip of Peninsular Malaysia, it is joined to the latter by the Johor-Singapore causeway carrying road and rail traffic.

Land is scarce, and the shape of the island has changed over the years through land reclamation. The highest point is Bukit Timah Hill at 162½ metres (580 ft) with most of the main island less than 15 metres (50 ft) above sea level.

Time

Singapore is 8 hours ahead of Greenwich Mean Time.

Tipping

You are not supposed to tip in Singapore, and in general this holds good, as most hotel bills come with a 10 percent service charge and 4 percent government tax. But if these are absent, tips are appreciated.

Tourist Information

There's a wealth of free leaflets and literature available in the airport, hotels and shopping centres, all making life easy for the visitor, giving details of what to do and how to do it. The **Singapore Tourist Promotion Board** has two Information Counters:

#01-19 Raffles City (8.30 a.m. - 5 p.m. Mon to Fri, 8.30 a.m. - 1 p.m. Sat). Tel: 330-0432

#02-02/03 Scotts Shopping Centre (9.30 a.m. - 9.30 p.m. daily) Tel: 738-3778

Personalised Tours

It is not easy to find anyone who knows more about Singapore than **Geraldine Lowe-Ismail**. She can tailor tours to wherever you please, on foot, by taxi or in a bus.

Her tours are fascinating, as she introduces you to all kinds of people in different parts of the island, giving full and detailed explanations.

She is a busy lady, and often out between 8 a.m. and 8 p.m. but you can phone (737-5250) to make arrangements in the evening or early morning. She charges S$60 for an hour of her time, but if you are lucky, you might be able to join a tour she has already organised. It would cost less, perhaps about S$20 - S$25 for half a day. Taxi hire with her would cost about S$22 for an hour, buses can be hired for a minimum period of 3 hours.

Geraldine is a fount of information, and a morning with her can really open your eyes.

Cultural Shows

Traditional Chinese, Indian and Malay dance performances are given at 11.45 a.m. in the Merlion Ballroom at the **Cockpit Hotel.** You will pay S$5, inclusive of a drink. After that, you can have a traditional Rijstaffel lunch, a variety of Indonesian dishes served with rice, in the Traveller's Palm restaurant. This costs S$15++. In the evening you can watch the show after a continental buffet dinner for S$30++, which is served between 7 and 8 p.m. The show begins at 8 p.m. and lasts three quarters of an hour. Both are held in the Merlion Ballroom.

The **Mandarin SIngapore** also holds a cultural show after a poolside barbeque buffet at 8 p.m. every night for $39++.

If you prefer not to dine, then enjoy a delicious Singapore Sling for just S$14 as you sit back and watch the graceful movements of the Oriental dances. For reservations, call 734-2001.

How Not To Offend

Good behaviour in Singapore is law enforced, clear signs explain what to do and what not to do. Littering could cost you up to S$1,000; smoking in government offices, airconditioned restaurants, cinemas, supermarkets etc., S$500; and if you're caught without a seat belt you'll pay S$50.

You won't be fined, but remember to take off your shoes when you enter a mosque or Indian temple or an Asian's house. When with Muslims, neither eat nor offer anything with your left hand.

In general Singapore is cosmopolitan, and courteous behaviour will make sure you don't offend, even if you are unfamiliar with the finer points of Asian etiquette. To learn more, look out for a fascinating book by Jo Ann Craig called *Culture Shock in Singapore and Malaysia* which explains the mores.

GETTING AROUND

Car Hire

If you feel like the independence of driving, **Avis** (Tel: 737-1668) offers self-drive cars from S$134 to S$439 for a 24-hour period. You will need an international driving licence. A chauffeur-driven mercedes costs S$60 per hour.

Parking coupons, and Central Business District (CBD) coupons to be displayed on the windscreen (required between 7.30 -10.15 a.m. weekdays and Saturdays, and 4.30 - 6.30 p.m. on weekdays if driving into the restricted zone) must be purchased at any one of the kiosks located around Singapore.

Taxis

By far the easiest way to see Singapore is to take one of the more than 10,000 taxis here. They provide excellent and very reasonable service. S$3 is added to the me-

PLEASE DO NOT LITTER
LITTERING CARRIES A MAXIMUM FINE OF $1000

ter fare for a trip from Changi Airport. During the CBD operating period a sticker must be displayed, which costs the passenger S$3 extra. A surcharge of S$1 for leaving the CBD is also imposed between 4 and 7 p.m. on weekdays, and noon to 3 p.m. on Saturdays. Calling a taxi costs S$2 extra, and a booking S$3.

Buses

Sometimes confusing, but timetables are sold in leading bookshops and bus terminals, and indicate the buses to and from the main attractions. The system is good and cheap, with fares starting at 50 cents.

MRT

Singapore's spanking new underground Mass Rapid Transit System is the envy of Londoners. Strict laws and fines prohibiting eating and littering ensure spotless stations and carriages. The system is efficient and

simple to use, just remember you need your ticket to leave the station at your destination.

Trishaws

Although mainly used by tourist groups, you can simply hire a trishaw, but make sure you agree on the destination and fare first.

Boats

Boat tours may be joined at **Collyer Quay** and the **World Trade Centre** for trips out to the islands. Arrange the length of time and cost before you set out, and expect to pay about S$25 to S$30 per hour.

Chartering luxury yachts has become more popular recently, and if you can make up a party, you can choose your own itinerary and sail in style, enquiries to **Amaril Cruises**, Tel: 221-6969.

Maps

There are several excellent free maps which have detailed sections of specific parts of the city, like Chinatown. These can be picked up at the Airport and major hotels. Most bookshops stock larger maps of Singapore and Malaysia.

Then there's the *Secret Map of Singapore* which give colourful and graphical summaries of the major places of interest in Singapore, such as temples and food centres.

WHERE TO STAY

Hotels

There is an enormous selection of hotels in Singapore, ranging from some of the best in the world to quite cheap accommodation. The prices below are for the least expensive single room and a deluxe suite. The rates quoted are subject to a 10 percent service charge and 4 percent government tax.

S+NUMBER indicates the postal district.

About S$300 and up

Shangri-La Hotel
2 Orange Grove Road, S.1025.
Tel: 737-3644
S$300 - S$1,000

Oriental Hotel
6 Raffles Blvd., S.0923.
Tel: 338-0066
S$295 - S$1,190

Omni Marco Polo
247 Tanglin Road, S.1024.
Tel: 474-7141
S$300 - S$750

Goodwood Park Hotel
22 Scotts Road, S.0922.

Tel: 737-7411
S$355 - S$1,100

S$200 and up

Pan Pacific Hotel
Marina Square, 7 Raffles Blvd., S.0103.
S$260 - S$640

York Hotel
21 Mount Elizabeth, S.0922.
Tel: 737-0511
S$220 - S$590

S$150 and up

Novotel Orchid Singapore
214 Dunearn Road, S.1129.
Tel: 250-3322
S$180 - S$800

Hotel Equatorial
429 Bukit Timah Road, S.1025.
Tel: 732-0431
S$160 - S$280

Hotel Phoenix
Orchard Rd./Somerset Rd., S.0923.
Tel: 737-8666
S$160 - S$300

S$100 and up

Garden Hotel
14 Balmoral Road, S.1025.
Tel: 235-3344
S$140 - S$280

Ladyhill Hotel
1 Ladyhill Road, S.1025.
Tel: 737-2111
S$140 - S$300

Hotel Premier
22 Nassim Rd., S.1025.
Tel: 733-9811
S$120 - S$180

THE ORIENTAL

Hotel Asia
37 Scotts Road, S.0922.
Tel: 737-8388
S$120 - S$210

Strand Hotel
25 Bencoolen Street, S.0718.
Tel: 338-1866
S$110 - S$160

RELC International House
30 Orange Grove Road, S.1025.
Tel: 737-9044
S$102 - S$130

Under S$100

Sloane Court Hotel
17 Balmoral Road, S.1025.
Tel: 235-3311
S$96.80 no suites

Metropolitan YMCA
60 Stevens Road, S.1025.
Tel: 737-7755
S$62 - S$103

Orchard YMCA
1 Orchard Road, S.0922.
Tel: 337344
S$60.50 - S$99

Service Apartments

The Ascott
6 Scotts Road, S.0922.
Tel: 732-0033
Daily rate: S$175 - S$650; monthly
S$4,200 - S$15,000

HEALTH AND EMERGENCIES

Health

Singapore's water is treated and safe for drinking, and the clean,

green image is a fact. Strict control is exercised over eating places from hawker stalls to hotels, and unless you over indulge in chillies there should be no problem. However, if you need a hospital, there are nine government hospitals and several private hospitals as well as umpteen clinics for any eventuality. Consultation fees start at about S$25 in a private practice, and it is a good idea to phone your embassy for a recommendation.

Emergencies

In an emergency dial 999 for the police, and 995 for the fire brigade or ambulance service.

HOURS OF BUSINESS

Business Hours

Business hours are from 9 a.m. until 5 p.m. and banks are open from 10 a.m. until 3 p.m. on weekdays, and from 9.30 a.m. to 11.30 a.m. on Saturdays.

The General Post Office in Fullerton Building operates from 8 a.m. to 6 p.m. on weekdays and till 4 p.m. on Saturdays; closed Sundays.

Branch post offices open from 8.30 a.m. to 5 p.m. on weekdays and from 8.30 a.m. to 2 or 4 p.m. on Saturdays. Branch offices are open till 8 p.m. on one weekday night.

There are two **24-hour post offices**, one in the annex to the General Post Office, and one in the Comcentre, 31 Exeter Road.

Shops open at about 10 a.m. until 6 p.m. and many department stores are open until 9 p.m. Most shops open on Sundays too.

PUBLIC HOLIDAYS IN 1991

New Year's Day: January 1
Chinese New Year: February 15 & 16
Good Friday: March 29
Hari Raya Puasa: April 16
Labour Day: May 1
Vesak Day: May 2
National Day: August 9
Hari Raya Haji: Sunday June 23, Public Holiday: June 24
Deepavali: November 5
Christmas Day: December 25

COMMUNICATIONS AND NEWS

Telecommunication and Postal Services

Singapore is completely up to date and efficient in telecommunications. Most hotels and offices have fax machines, and almost every hotel room has an IDD phone, with 004 or 005 being the international code.

Public telephones are easily available, and costs 10 cents for every 3 minutes for local calls. Clearly marked phones can be used for world-wide calls. To avoid running out of coins in the midst of a conversation, buy $2,

$10, $20 or $50 phone cards, usable for both local and overseas calls.

Postal services are fast and efficient. An aerogram to anywhere in the world costs 35 cents; a registered item S$2, and just add S$1.50 for express mail. Most hotels handle mail or you may post letters and parcels yourself at the General Post Office.

Newspapers

The Straits Times and *The Business Times* are local English language dailies, carrying detailed local news as well as international coverage, with the tabloid *New Paper* appearing in the afternoons. *The International Herald Tribune* is available on the day of publication, arriving by fax from Paris and printed here, and from Britain *The International Express* is faxed from London and also printed here.

Radio

The Singapore Broadcasting Corporation's (SBC) English channels are Radio 1 (90.5 MHz) and Radio 10 (98.7 MHz), the general channels, Radio 5 (92.4 MHz) has classical music, Class 95 FM (95 MHz) has contemporary music, and the BBC World Service is on 88.9 MHz. Two stations from Batam, on 100.7 and 101.6 MHz, broadcast English and some Indonesian pop

Television

SBC's Channel 5 broadcasts the news, dramas and sit-coms in all four official languages while Channel 12 has more cultural programs such as Pavarotti in Concert. Channels 3 and 10 and TV3 can be received from Malaysia.

SPORTS

Singaporeans are a healthy lot, smoking is discouraged (or prohibited at most restaurants), although there is plenty of *yam seng*ing (cheers! bottoms up!) of brandy at Chinese banquets. They like to keep fit, be it in the gym or jogging in the park, so sporty types should feel quite at home here.

Golf is extremely popular and there are 10 clubs with plenty of beautiful courses. Most parks have jogging tracks and there are tennis, squash and badminton courts, but in this climate, you may prefer the swimming pool or the exhilarating water sports like windsurfing or waterskiing.

Most hotels have pools and fitness centres and many have tennis facilities too.

Golf

Green fees range from S$40 for a 9-hole course on weekdays to S$200 for a full round at a championship course at the weekend. Club rental costs about S$15 - S$20.

Changi Golf Club, Netheravon Road. 9 holes. Tel: 545-1298.

Jurong Country Club, Jurong Town Hall Road. 18 holes. Tel: 560-5655.

Keppel Club, Bukit Chermin. 18 holes. Tel: 273-5522.

Raffles Country Club, 450 Jalan Ahmad Ibrahim. Two 18-hole courses. Tel: 861-7655.

Seletar Country Club, Seletar Airbase. 9 holes. Tel: 481-4746.

Sembawang Country Club, 10½ Miles, Sembawang Road. 18 holes. Tel: 257-0642.

Sentosa Golf Club, Sentosa Island. Two 18-hole courses. Tel: 472-2722.

Singapore Island Country Club. Two locations, each with two 18-hole courses. Upper Thomson Road, Tel: 459-2222. 240 Sime Road, Tel: 466-2244.

Tanah Merah Country Club, Changi Coast Road. Two 18-hole courses. Tel: 542-3040.

Warren Golf Club, Folkestone Road. 9 holes. Tel: 777-6533.

There are several driving ranges, one of which is at **Parkland**, East Coast Parkway. 48 bays, 200-metre range, 90 balls for $5. 7.30 a.m. - 10 p.m. Tel: 440-6726.

Tennis

Booking a tennis court costs about S$6 per hour, more if you play in the evening under the lights.

Kallang Tennis Centre, Stadium Road. Tel: 348-1291.

Singapore Tennis Centre, East Coast Parkway. Tel: 442-5966.

Tanglin Tennis Centre, Sherwood Road. Tel: 473-7236.

Squash

Court bookings cost $3 - $6 per hour.

East Coast Recreation Centre. East Coast Parkway. Tel: 449-0541.

Farrer Park, Rutland Road. Tel: 251-4166.

National Stadium, Kallang. Tel: 348-1258.

Singapore Squash Centre, Fort Canning Rise. Tel: 336-0155.

Windsurfing

East Coast Sailing Centre, 1210 East Coast Parkway, Tel: 449-5118, offers a half-day course for $50, or a two-day course for $80. Laser sailing lessons are available on a laser single handed boat at S$270 for either a 4 x ½ day or a 2 x full-day course. A laser boat may be hired for S$20 an hour and a 6-man dingy for S$50 an hour.

Waterskiing

There are two locations for waterskiing, one for the beginner or social skier, and one which enables the practised skier to make use of a slalom course.

At Punggol. William Water Sports, 35 Punggol 24th Avenue. Tel: 282-6879. Here, skiing costs S$60 per hour which includes ski hire, boat, driver and petrol. This is the easier location and more fun if you make up a group.

Kallang. Pager: 600-4151. Here the cost is S$80 per hour for an outboard, or S$120 for an inboard tournament ski boat. You can also make 6 passes on the slalom course for S$25.

Canoeing

Canoes may be rented at S$3 for a single-seater and S$6 for a double-seater per hour.

East Coast Parkway, the Lagoon Food Centre.

Sentosa Lagoon, near the swimming lagoon.

Cycling

Bicycles may be hired at about 80 cents per hour, or S$1 for a BMX .

East Coast Parkway at bike-hire stalls.

Sentosa Island where there is a nearly 5-km (3 miles) track around the island.

Ice skating

At the **Fuji Ice Palace**, 2 Mackenzie Road, Tel: 336-2988.

Adults pay S$7 and children S$5 for 2 hours' skating at weekends; as long as you like in the week. Hire of skates costs S$2. The rink is open from 10 a.m. to 10 p.m.

Bowling

There are several alleys with games costing about S$3.50.

Kallang Bowler-Drome, 5 Stadium Walk. Tel: 345-0545.

Jackie's Bowl, 542B East Coast Road and 8 Grange Road. Tel: 241-6519 and 737-4744 respectively.

Plaza Bowl, Textile Centre, Jalan Sultan. Tel: 292-4821.

Super Bowl, Marina South. Tel: 221-1010.

Victor's Super Bowl, Marina South. Tel: 223-7998.

USEFUL ADDRESSES

Head Office:
Singapore Tourist Promotion Board (STPB)
Raffles City Tower, #32-01 250 North Bridge Road. S.0617. Tel: 339-6622 Telex: STBSIN RS 33375 Telefax: 339-0697 Cable:

TOURISPROM SINGAPORE
Open: Mondays-Fridays: 8.30 a.m. - 5 p.m. Saturdays: 8.30 a.m. - 1 p.m. (closed on Sundays & Public Holidays)
STPB Offices Overseas

ASIA
Hong Kong
Mr Loi Hai Poh
General Manager (North Asia)
Singapore Tourist Promotion Board (STPB)
Suite 1402, Century Square, 1-13, D'Aguilar Sheer Central, Hong Kong. Tel: 852-224052. Telex: 86-630 ETBHK HX Telefax: 852-8106694 Cable: TOURISPROM HONG KONG

Taipei
Mr Yeo Din Yew
General Manager (Taiwan)
Singapore Tourist Promotion Board
9th Floor, TFIT Tower, 85 Jen Ai Road, Section 4, Taipei, Taiwan. Tel: 721-0664. Tlx: 24-974 STPBTPE Cable: TOURISPROM TAIPEI

Tokyo
Mrs Elsie Chia-Ozaku
Regional Director (Japan)
Singapore Tourist Promotion Board
1st Floor, Yamato Seimei Building 1 Chome, 1-7 Uchisaiwai-cho Chiyoda-ku Tokyo 100, Japan
Tel: (03) 593-3388, Tlx: STBTYO J25591 Cable: TOURISPROM TOKYO Telefax: 3-591-1480

AUSTRALIA/NEW ZEALAND
Sydney
Chui Seng Wah
Director (Australia & NZ)
Singapore Tourist Promotion Board
Suite 1604, Level 16, Wespac Plaza, 60 Margaret St., Sydney NSW 2000,

Australia
Tel: 241-3771/2 Tlx: STBSYD AA
127-775 Cable: TOURISPROM
SYDNEY Telefax: (02) 232-3658

Perth
Magdalene Lee
General Manager (Western
Australia)
Singapore Tourist Promotion Board
8th Floor, St. George's Court,16 St.
George's Terrace, Perth WA 6000,
Australia Tel: (09) 325-8578/325-
8511 Tlx: AA 197542 Telefax: (09)
221-3864

Auckland
Mr Rodney Walshe (Representative)
Singapore Tourist Promotion Board
c/o Walshe's World, 2nd Floor
Dingwall Building, 87 Queen St. P.
O. Box 279, Auckland 1, New
Zealand. Tel: (9) 793-708 Tlx:
WALWOR NZ 21-437 Telefax: (09)
302-2420

EUROPE
Frankfurt
Mr Christopher Khoo
General Manager (Germany)
Singapore Tourist Promotion Board
(Fremdenverkehrsburo von Singa-
pur) Poststrasse 2-4 D-6000 Frank-
furt/Main Federal Republic of
Germany. Tel: (069) 231-456/7
Tlx: STBF D418-9742 Cable:
TOURISPROM FRANKFURT
Telefax: (069) 233924

London
Mr David C. P. Lee
Regional Director (United
Kingdom)
Singapore Tourist Promotion Board
1st Floor, Carrington House, 126-
130 Regent St., London W1R 5FE,
United Kingdom. Tel: (071) 437-
0033 Tlx: STBLON G 893-491

Cable: TOURISPROM LONDON
Telefax: (071) 734-2191

Paris
Mr Richard Ng
Regional Director (France)
Singapore Tourist Promotion Board
L'Office National du Tourisme de
Singapour, Centre d'Affaires Le
Louvre, 2 Place du Palais-Royal
75044 Paris Cedex 01 France. Tel:
4297.16.16 Tlx: SINGPAR 213-
593F Cable: TOURISPROM PARIS
Telefax: 4297-16-17

Zurich
Mr Ulrich Schellenberg
(Representative)STPB
(Fremdenverkehrsburo Von
Singapur) Hoinstrasse 48, CH-8044,
Zurich, Switzerland Tel: (01) 252-
5365 Tlx: 816464 SOMZH CH
Cable: TOURISPROM ZURICH

USA
Los Angeles
Mr Charles Leong
Senior Vice-President (Ametics)
Singapore Tourist Promotion
Board, 8484 Wilshire Boulevard,
Suite 510 Beverly Hills, CA 90211,
U.S.A.Tel: (213) 852-1901 Telex:
SING UR 278-141 Telefax: (213)
852-0129

New York
Mr Marc Tay Chew Liang
Vice-President (Eastern Region)
Singapore Tourist Promotion Board
590 Fifth Avenue, 12th Floor, New
York N.Y. 10036. Tel: (212) 302-
4861. Tlx: SING UR 220-843
Cable: TOURISPROM NEW YORK
Telefax: (212) 302-4801

Banks

Algemene Bank Nederland NY
18 Church St., S.0104.
Tel: 535-5511

Asia Commercial Bank Ltd
60 Robinson Road, S.0106.
Tel: 222-8222

Ban Hin Lee Bank
15 Phillip St. #01-00,
Tan Ean Kiam Bldg., S.0104.
Tel: 533-7022

Banque Nationale de Paris
20 Collyer Quay #01-01,
Tung Centre, S.0104.
Tel: 224-0211

Bangkok Bank
180 Cecil St.,
Bangkok Bank Bldg., S.0106.
Tel: 221-9400

Bank Negara Indonesia 1946
158 Cecil Street, S.0106.
Tel: 225-7755

Bank of America
78 Shenton Way,
Ong Bldg., S.0207.
Tel: 223-6688

Bank of China
4 Battery Road, S.0104.
Tel: 535-2411

Bank of East Asia
137 Market St., S.0104.
Tel: 224-1334

Bank of India
108 Robinson Road, S.0106.
Tel: 222-0011

Bank of Singapore
101 Cecil St. #01-02, S.0106.

Tel: 223-9266

Bank of Tokyo
16 Raffles Quay #01-06,
Hong Leong Bldg., S.0104.
Tel: 220-8111

Banque Indosuez
3 Shenton Way,
Shenton House, S.0106.
Tel: 220-7111

Chase Manhattan Bank
50 Raffles Place Shell Tower,
S.0104.
Tel: 530-4111

Chung Khiaw Bank
10 Anson Road #01-01,
International Plaza, S.0207.
Tel: 222-8622

Citibank N A
1 Shenton Way #17-05,
Robina House, S.0106.
Tel: 225-5225

Development Bank of Singapore
6 Shenton Way, DBS Bldg., S.0106.
Tel: 220-1111

Far Eastern Bank
156 Cecil St.,
Far Eastern Bldg., S.0106.
Tel: 221-9055

Four Seas Bank
19-25 Cecil St., S.0104.
Tel: 224-9898

Hong Kong & Shanghai Banking Corpn
10 Collyer Quay #01-01,
Ocean Bldg., S.0104.
Tel: 530-5000

Indian Overseas Bank
IDB Building, 64 Cecil St., S.0104.
Tel: 225-1100

Industrial & Commercial Bank
2 Shenton Way #01-01,
ICB Bldg., S.0106.
Tel: 221-1711

International Bank of Singapore
50 Collyer Quay, #02-01,
Overseas Union House, S.0104.
Tel: 223-4488

Kwangtung Provincial Bank
60 Cecil St., Kwangtung Provincial
Bank Bldg., S.0104.
Tel: 223-9622

Lee Wah Bank
1 Shenton Way #01-03, Robina
House, S.0106.
Tel: 225-8844

Malayan Banking Berhad
2 Battery Road #01-00, Malayan
Bank Chamber, S.0104.
Tel: 535-2266

Oversea-Chinese Banking Corpn
65 Chulia St., OCBC Centre,
S.0104.
Tel: 535-7222

Overseas Union Bank
1 Raffles Place, OUB Centre,
S.0104.Tel: 533-8686

Security Pacific National Bank
50 Raffles Place #01-03, Shell
Towers, S.0104.
Tel: 224-3363

Societe Generale de Banque
105 Cecil St. #20-01/04, The
Octagon, S.0106.
Tel: 533-8686

Standard Chartered Bank
6 Battery Road, S.0104.
Tel: 225-8888

Tat Lee Bank
63 Market St. Tat Lee Bank Bldg.,
S.0104.
Tel: 533-9292

UCO Bank
2 D'Almeida St., Bharat Bldg.,
S.0104.
Tel: 532-5944

**United Malayan Banking Corpn
Berhad**
150 Cecil St., #01-00, Wing On Life
Bldg., S.0106
Tel: 225-3111

United Overseas Bank
1 Bonham St., Raffles Place, S.0104.
Tel: 533-9898

Airlines

Aeroflot Soviet Airlines
15 Queen St. #01-02,
Tan Chong Tower, S.0718.
Tel: 336-1757

Air India
5 Shenton Way #17-01,
UIC Bldg., S.0106.
Tel: 225-9411

Air Mauritius
135 Cecil St. #01-00,
LKN Bldg., S.0106.
Tel: 222-3033

Air Nauru
10 Anson Road #01-57,
International Plaza, S.0207.
Tel: 222-6738

Air New Zealand
10 Collyer Quay #07-05,
Ocean Bldg., S.0104.
Tel: 535-8266

Air Niugini
Thomson Road #01-05/06,
United Square, S.1130.
Tel: 250-4868

Royal Jordanian Airline
15 Beach Road #03-11,
Beach Centre, S.0718.
Tel: 338-8188

Alitalia
435 Orchard Road, #15-04,
Wisma Atria, S.0923.
Tel: 737-6966

Biman Bangladesh Airlines
15 McCallum St. #01-02,
Nat West Centre, S.0106.
Tel: 221-7155

British Airways
#02-16 The Paragon, S.0923.
Tel: 253-8444

Cathay Pacific Airways
10 Collyer Quay #16-01,
Ocean Bldg., S.0104.
Tel: 533-1333

China Airlines
#01-02 Orchard Tower,
Orchard Rd., S.0923.
Tel: 737-2211

Czechoslovak Airlines
25 Scotts Road #04-05,
Royal Holiday Inn, S.0922.
Tel: 737-9844

Finnair
541 Orchard Road #08-01,
Liat Towers, S.0923.
Tel: 733-3377

Garuda Indonesia Airways
101 Thomson Road #13-03,
United Square, S.1130.
Tel: 250-2888

Japan Airlines (JAL)
16 Raffles Quay #01-01,
Hong Leong Bldg., S.0104.
Tel: 221-0522

KLM Royal Dutch Airlines
333 Orchard Road #01-02,
Mandarin Hotel Arcade, S.0923.
Tel: 737-7622

Korean Airlines
Collyer Quay #01-02,
Ocean Bldg., S.0104.
Tel: 534-2111

Lufthansa German Airlines
19 Tanglin Road #03-01,
Tanglin Shopping Centre, S.1023.
Tel: 737-9222

Malaysian Airlines System (MAS)
190 Clemenceau Avenue #02-09,
Singapore Shopping Centre, S.0923.
Tel: 336-6777

Olympic Airways
16 Raffles Quay #15-04,
Hong Leong Bldg., S.0104.
Tel: 225-8877

Pakistan International Airlines
101 Thomson Road #01-01,
United Square S.1130.
Tel: 251-2322

Philippine Airlines
35 Selegie Road #10-02,
Parklane Shopping Mall, S.0718
Tel: 336-1611

Qantas Airways
#04-02 The Promenade, S.0923.
Tel: 737-3744

Royal Brunei Airlines
25 Scotts Road #01-4A/4B/5,
Royal Holiday Inn Shopping Centre,
S.0922.

Tel: 235-4672

Sabena World Airlines
10 Anson Road #01-31,
International Plaza, S.0207.
Tel: 221-6081

Saudi Arabian Airlines
7500A Beach Road #10-318,
The Plaza, S.0719.
Tel: 291-7322

Scandinavian Airlines System
#23-01/04 Gateway East,
152 Beach Road, S.0718.
Tel: 294-1611

Singapore Airlines (SIA)
77 Robinson Road, S.0106.
Tel: 223-8888/545-6666

Swissair
304 Orchard Road #03-18,
Lucky Plaza, S.0923.
Tel: 737-8133

Tarom Romanian Air Transport
3 Coleman St. #03-07/08,
Peninsula Shopping Complex,
S.0617.
Tel: 338-1467

Thai Airways International
133 Cecil St. #08-01,
Keck Seng Towers, S.0106.
Tel: 224-9977

United Airlines
16 Raffles Quay #44-00,
Hong Leong Bldg., S.0104.
Tel: 220-0711

UTA French Airlines
400 Orchard Road #14-05,
Orchard Towers, S.0923.
Tel: 737-6355

Yugoslav Airlines (JAT)
541 Orchard Road #02-03,
Liat Towers, S.0923.
Tel: 235-3017

Airlines with offices in Singapore

Air Canada
100 Orchard Road #02-43/46,
Meridien Shopping Centre, S.0923.
Tel: 732-8555

Air France
400 Orchard Road #14-05,
Orchard Towers, S.0923.
Tel: 737-7166

Airlanka
140 Cecil St. #02-00/B,
PIL Bldg., S.0106.
Tel: 223-6026

American Airlines Inc
15 McCallum St. #11-02,
Natwest Centre, S.0105.
Tel: 221-6988

Northwest Airlines
435 Orchard Rd. #11-03,
Wisma Atria, S.0923.
Tel: 235-7166

Trans World Airlines (TWA)
7500A Beach Road #09-324,
The Plaza, S.0719.
Tel: 293-6833

Turkish Airlines
545 Orchard Road #02-21,
Far East Shopping Centre, S.0923.
Tel: 732-4556

USEFUL TELEPHONE NUMBERS

Fire, Ambulance   995
Police   999

Flight Information 542-5680
Meteorological
(forecast) Office 542-7788
Postal Service 165
Telephone Directory Assistance
103
Assistance in Calling (local calls)
100
Time Announcing Service 1711
Singapore Bus Service 287-2727
Singapore Tourist
Promotion Board 235-6611
Railway Administration 222-5165
Overseas Call Booking 104

Embassies and Consulates

Argentina
302 Orchard Road #10-04, Tong
Bldg., S.0923.
Tel: 235-4231
Open: 9 a.m.- 3 p.m., Mon-Fri.

Australia
25 Napier Road, S.1025.
Tel: 737-9311
Mon-Fri.

Austria
1 Scotts Road #22-04,
Shaw Centre, S.0922.
Tel: 235-4088
Open: 8 a.m.- 4 p.m., Mon-Fri.

Bangladesh
101 Thomson Road #06-07,
United Square, S.1130.
Tel: 255-0075/250-5539
Open: 9 a.m.- 5 p.m., Mon-
Fri.(Closed: 1 p.m.-2 p.m.)

Belgium
10 Anson Road #09-24,
International Plaza, S.0207.
Tel: 220-7677
Open: 8.30 a.m.- 12.30 p.m., 1.30
p.m.- 4 p.m., Mon-Fri.

Brazil
302 Orchard Road #15-03/04,
Tong Bldg., S.0923.
Tel: 734-3435
Open: 10 a.m.- 1 p.m., 2 p.m. - 5
p.m., Mon-Fri.

Britain
Tanglin Road, S.1024.
Tel: 473-9333
Open: 9.00 a.m.-12 p.m., 2 p.m.- 4
p.m., Mon-Fri.

Brunei
7A Tanglin Hill, S.1024.
Tel: 474-3393
Open: 8.30 a.m. - 12.30 p.m., 1.30
p.m. - 4.30 p.m., Mon-Thur.; 8.30
a.m. - 12 p.m., 2.30 p.m.- 4.30 p.m.,
Fri.

Bulgaria
15 Scotts Road #09-09, Thong
Teck Bldg., S.0922.
Tel: 737-1111
Open: 9 a.m.- 12 p.m., 1.30 p.m.-
5 p.m., Mon-Fri.

Burma
15 St. Martin Drive, S.1025.
Tel: 235-8704
Open: 9 a.m.- 5 p.m., Mon-
Fri.(Closed: 1 p.m.- 2 p.m.)

Canada
80 Anson Road, 14th & 15th Storey,
IBM Towers, S.0207.
Tel: 2256363
Open: 8 a.m.- 12.30 p.m., 1.30
p.m.- 4.30 p.m. Mon-Fri.

Chilean Embassy
105 Cecil Street #14-01,
The Octagon, S.0106.
Tel: 2238577
Open: 9 a.m.- 2 p.m., Mon-Fri.

Cyprus, Consulate of the Republic of
6 Kung Chong Road, S.0315.
Tel: 4748473
Open: 9.30 a.m.- 12.30 p.m., 2 p.m.- 5 p.m., Mon-Fri.

Denmark
101 Thomson Road #13-01/02, United Square, S.1130.
Tel: 250-3383
Open: 8.30 a.m.- 4 p.m., Mon-Thurs, 8.30 a.m.- 1.30 p.m. Fri.

Egypt
75 Grange Road, S.2775.
Tel: 737-1811
Open: 9 a.m.- 3 p.m., Mon-Fri.

Finland
101 Thomson Road #21-02/03, United Square, S.1130.
Tel: 254-4042
Open: 8.30 a.m.- 12.30 p.m., 1 p.m.- 4 p.m.,
Mon-Fri.

France
5 Gallop Road, S.1025.
Tel: 466-4866
Open: 9 a.m.-1 p.m., 2 p.m.- 4 p.m., Mon-Fri.

Germany (Federal Republic of)
545 Orchard Road #14-01, Far East Shopping Centre, S.0923.
Tel: 737-1355
Open: 8 a.m.- 4 p.m., Mon-Thur, 8 a.m.- 2 p.m., Fri.(Closed: 1 p.m.- 2 p.m., except Fri.)

Greece
51 Anson Road #11-51, Anson Centre, S.0207.
Tel: 220-8622
Open: 9 a.m.- 5 p.m., Mon-Fri.(Closed: 1 p.m.-2 p.m.); 9 a.m.-1 p.m., Sat.

Hungary
101 Thomson Road #22-05, United Square, S.1130.
Tel: 250-4424/250-9215
Open: 9.30 a.m.- 4.30 p.m., Mon-Fri.

India
31 Grange Road, S.2775.
Tel: 737-6777
Open: 9 a.m.- 5 p.m., Mon-Fri.(Closed: 1 p.m.-1.30 p.m.)

Indonesia
7 Chatsworth Road, S.1024
Tel: 737-7422
Open: 8.30 a.m.- 12.30 p.m., 2 p.m.- 4.30 p.m., Mon-Fri.

Ireland
541 Orchard Road #08-02, Liat Towers, S.0923.
Tel: 732-3430
Open: 9 a.m.- 5 p.m., Mon-Fri; 9 a.m.- 12.30 p.m.

Israel
230 Orchard Road #11-230, Faber House, S.0923.
Tel: 235-0966
Open: 8.30 a.m.- 4.30 p.m., Mon-Thur. Closed on Fri. at 3.30 p.m.

Italy
101 Thomson Road #27-02/03, United Square, S.1130.
Tel: 250-6022
Open: 8.30 a.m.- 1.30 p.m., Mon-Fri.

Japan
16 Nassim Road, S.1025.
Tel: 235-8855
Open: 8.30 a.m.- 4.30 p.m., Mon, Tues, Thur, Fri (Closed 12.30 p.m.- 2 p.m.); 8.30 a.m.- 12.30 p.m.,Wed, Sat.

Korea (Democratic People's Republic of)
19 Fort Road, S.1543.
Tel: 345-3044
Open: 9.30 a.m.- 5.30 p.m., Mon-Fri. (Closed: 12 p.m.-2 p.m.)

Korea (Republic of)
101 Thomson Road #10-03,
United Square, S.1130
Tel: 256-1188
Open: 8.30 a.m.- 12.30 p.m., 2 p.m.-4.30 p.m., Mon-Fri; 8.30 a.m.-12.30 p.m., Sat.

Malaysia
301 Jervois Road, S.1024.
Tel: 235-0011
Open: 8.30 a.m.- 12 p.m., 2.45 p.m.-3.15 p.m., Mon-Fri.; 8.30 a.m.- 12 p.m., Sat.

Netherlands
541 Orchard Road #13-01,
Liat Towers, S.0923.
Tel: 737-1155
Open: 9 a.m.- 12 p.m.,1.30 p.m.- 3 p.m., Mon-Fri.

New Zealand
13 Nassim Road, S.1025.
Tel: 235-9966
Open: 8.30 a.m.- 12.30 p.m., 1.30 p.m.- 4.30 p.m., Mon-Fri.

Norway
16 Raffles Quay #44-01,
Hong Leong Bldg., S.0104.
Tel: 220-7122
Open: 9 a.m.- 4 p.m., Mon-Fri.

Pakistan
20A Nassim Road, S.1025.
Tel: 737-6988
Open: 9 a.m.- 5 p.m., Mon-Fri. (Closed:1 p.m.-2 p.m.)

Panama
16 Raffles Quay #41-06,
Hong Leong Bldg., S.0104.
Tel: 221-8677
Open: 9 a.m.- 4.30 p.m., Mon-Fri, (Closed 12 p.m.- 2 p.m.)

Peru
7 Brookvale Drive #03-11,
Edale Block, S.2159.
Tel: 4670497
Open: 9 a.m.- 4 p.m., Mon-Fri; 9 a.m.- 1 p.m., Sat.

Philippines
20B Nassim Road, S.1025.
Tel: 737-3977
Open: 9 a.m.- 12 p.m., 2 p.m.- 4.30 p.m., Mon-Fri.

Poland
100 Beach Road # 33-11/12,
Shaw Towers, S.0718.
Tel: 294-2513
Open: 9 a.m.- 4 p.m., Mon-Fri.

Romania
48 Jalan Harom Setangkai, S.1025.
Tel: 468-3424
Open: 8 a.m.- 4 p.m., Mon-Fri; 8 a.m.- 12 p.m., Sat.

Saudi Arabia
10 Nassim Road, S.1025.
Tel: 734-5878
Open: 8.30 a.m.- 4 p.m., Mon-Fri. (Closed: 12 p.m.- 2.30 p.m., Fri.)

Spain
15 Scotts Rd., #05-08/09,
Thong Teck Bldg., S.0923.
Tel: 732-9788
Open: 9.30 a.m.- 1 p.m., 2.30 p.m. - 5 p.m., Mon-Fri.

Sri Lanka
51 Newton Road #13-07,
Goldhill Plaza, S.1130.

Tel: 254-4595
Open: 9 a.m.- 1 p.m., 2 p.m.- 5.15
p.m., Mon-Fri.

Sweden
111 Somerset Road #05-08,
PUB Bldg,
Devonshire Wing, S.0923.
Tel: 734-2771
Open: 8.30 a.m.- 12 p.m., 2 p.m.-
4 p.m., Mon-Fri.

Switzerland
1 Swiss Club Link, S.0923.
Tel: 68-5788
Open: 9 a.m.- 1 p.m., Mon-Fri.

Thailand
370 Orchard Road, S.0923.
Tel: 737-2644
Open: 9 a.m.- 12.30 p.m., 2 p.m.-
5 p.m., Mon-Fri.

Turkey
20B Nassim Road, S.1025.
Tel: 7329211
Open: 9.30 a.m.- 12 p.m., 2 p.m.-
5 p.m., Mon-Fri.

USA
30 Hill St., S.0617.
Tel: 338-0251
Open: 8.30 a.m.- 12 p.m., Mon-Fri.

USSR
51 Nassim Road, S.1025.
Tel: 235-1834
Open: 10 a.m.- 12 p.m., Mon-Fri.

FURTHER READING

Jane Beamish & Jane Ferguson: *A
History of Singapore Architecture,
The Making of a City*. Graham
Brash.

Text by Sumiko Tan, Photographs
by Michael Liew: *Streets of Old
Chinatown Singapore*. Page Media.

Historical

Noel Barber: *Sinister Twilight*.
Coronet. Fascinating account of the
fall of Singapore.

*Straits Affairs. The Malay World
and Singapore*. "Being Glimpses of
the Straits Settlements and the
Malay Peninsula in the Nineteenth
Century as seen through the
Illustrated London News and other
contemporary sources." Compiled
by J.M. Tate. John Nicholson Ltd.

Historical Fiction

Noel Barber: *Tanamera*. Coronet.
Good read, fiction set in the period
above.

Goh Sin Tub: *The Nan-mei-su
Girls of Emerald Hill*. Heinemann
Asia. Local writer, story set in
Emerald Hill during the war.

Classics

Joseph Conrad: *Lord Jim*.
Penguin.

Anthony Burgess: *The Malayan
Trilogy*. Penguin. Not strictly
Singapore but a must for those in-
terested in this part of the world.

Somerset Maugham: *Collected
Short Stories*. Mandarin. More
Malaya, but a fascinating insight in-
to life in the colonies.

Local Fiction

Philip Jeyeratnam: *First Loves.* Times Books International. Growing up in Singapore, an interesting insight by a prize-winning author.

Catherine Lim: *Little Ironies, Stories of Singapore.* Heinemann Asia.
Ups and downs of Singapore life recounted with great perception.

Catherine Lim: *O Singapore!* Times Books International. Very amusing and penetrating look at Singapore today.

Guidebooks

Insight Guide: Singapore. APA Publications.

Lesley Layton: *Cultures of the World. Singapore.* Times Books International

More on Singapore

David Brazil: *Street Smart Singapore.* Times Books International.

The Secret Map of Singapore. Ropion, Blaisdell, Mowe.

Singapore's 100 Best Restaurants 1991. Compiled by the Editors of Singapore Tatler. Illustrated Magazine Publishing Co. Ltd.

BIBLIOGRAPHY

Ministry of Communications and Information: *Singapore Facts and Figures 1990* and *Singapore 1990.*

Norman Edwards & Peter Keys: *Singapore, A Guide to Buildings, Streets, Places.* Times Books International.

C.M.Turnbull: *A History of Singapore 1819 - 1975.* Oxford University Press.

ART/ PHOTO CREDITS

Photography by **Ingo Jezierski**

Cover Design **Klaus Geisler**

Maps **Berndtson & Berndtson**

Index

Cheers !
Perfected in Pewterware

TUMASEK PEWTER

NOTES